Human Behavior and Another Kind in Consciousness:

Emerging Research and Opportunities

Shigeki Sugiyama
Independent Researcher, Japan

A volume in the Advances in Human
and Social Aspects of Technology
(AHSAT) Book Series

Published in the United States of America by
    IGI Global
    Information Science Reference (an imprint of IGI Global)
    701 E. Chocolate Avenue
    Hershey PA, USA 17033
    Tel: 717-533-8845
    Fax: 717-533-8661
    E-mail: cust@igi-global.com
    Web site: http://www.igi-global.com

Library of Congress Cataloging-in-Publication Data

Names: Sugiyama, Shigeki, 1952- author.
Title: Human behavior and another kind in consciousness : emerging research
  and opportunities / by Shigeki Sugiyama.
Description: Hershey, PA : Information Science Reference, [2019]
Identifiers: LCCN 2018049687| ISBN 9781522582175 (hardcover) | ISBN
  9781522582182 (ebook)
Subjects: LCSH: Human behavior. | Artificial intelligence. | Consciousness.
Classification: LCC BF199 .S84 2019 | DDC 153--dc23 LC record available at https://lccn.loc.
gov/2018049687

This book is published in the IGI Global book series Advances in Human and Social Aspects of Technology (AHSAT) (ISSN: 2328-1316; eISSN: 2328-1324)

British Cataloguing in Publication Data
A Cataloguing in Publication record for this book is available from the British Library.

All work contributed to this book is new, previously-unpublished material.
The views expressed in this book are those of the authors, but not necessarily of the publisher.

For electronic access to this publication, please contact: eresources@igi-global.com.

Advances in Human and Social Aspects of Technology (AHSAT) Book Series

ISSN:2328-1316
EISSN:2328-1324

Editor-in-Chief: Ashish Dwivedi, The University of Hull, UK

MISSION

In recent years, the societal impact of technology has been noted as we become increasingly more connected and are presented with more digital tools and devices. With the popularity of digital devices such as cell phones and tablets, it is crucial to consider the implications of our digital dependence and the presence of technology in our everyday lives.

The **Advances in Human and Social Aspects of Technology (AHSAT) Book Series** seeks to explore the ways in which society and human beings have been affected by technology and how the technological revolution has changed the way we conduct our lives as well as our behavior. The AHSAT book series aims to publish the most cutting-edge research on human behavior and interaction with technology and the ways in which the digital age is changing society.

COVERAGE

- Human Rights and Digitization
- Computer-Mediated Communication
- Human-Computer Interaction
- Public Access to ICTs
- Cyber Bullying
- Philosophy of technology
- Gender and Technology
- Digital Identity
- End-User Computing
- Cultural Influence of ICTs

IGI Global is currently accepting manuscripts for publication within this series. To submit a proposal for a volume in this series, please contact our Acquisition Editors at Acquisitions@igi-global.com or visit: http://www.igi-global.com/publish/.

Titles in this Series

For a list of additional titles in this series, please visit:
https://www.igi-global.com/book-series/advances-human-social-aspects-technology/37145

For an entire list of titles in this series, please visit:
https://www.igi-global.com/book-series/advances-human-social-aspects-technology/37145

701 East Chocolate Avenue, Hershey, PA 17033, USA
Tel: 717-533-8845 x100 • Fax: 717-533-8661
E-Mail: cust@igi-global.com • www.igi-global.com

Table of Contents

Preface

It is just now at the top of an aggregation point of globalization era in terms of things and living creatures. The communication methods including in many sorts of transfers like commodity, facility, information, system, thought, knowledge, people, culture, heritage, etc. may cause many kinds of and many types of interactions among us, which may have made the world closer but complex, smaller but intense, influential but solitude, networked but dividable, accumulated but distributed, direct but standstill, stable but chaotic, abstracted but differentiated loosely, many possibilities but almost none, free but controlled, unique but ubiquitous, solitude but mass, directed but diverge, and accumulated knowledge but ordinal. As the results of these situations, they may cause even an individual world much wider or smaller, closer or divided, quicker or slower, dependent or independent, massive or nothing, unique or ubiquitous, far expanded or shrunk, any opportunity expected or nothing desired, viewable or invisible, manageable or uncontrollable, simple or chaotic, and limited or borderless. As they are just observed, these phenomena in the world are being existed as an extreme opposite twin (Dipole and Pair) unit at the same time. This has been the causations of the Multi Dipoles. These phenomena of the Multi Dipoles have caused the situations of many kinds of Mini Clouds by being used of the Information Technology (IT) for offering necessary and desired information to us individually. These phenomena of the Multi Dipoles seem to be further deepened and extended under these phenomena of the dipoles. But on the contrary, these phenomena will turn out to be the opposite direction. Namely, these phenomena will make the Multi Dipoles converge into Unique Dipole in the very near future as the public usages will go to the two kinds of categories (groups) of people; Simple Users and Controlled Venders.

Talking about the functions of Mini Clouds in the same flow, it will become possible to access seamlessly to any Mini Cloud whose phenomenon will make the Mini Clouds converge into the Unique Cloud. Under these situations and conditions, an individual person will be able to get a thing and information as many as and as much as being wanted in order to accomplish one's desire. And it will be very easy to do. But on the other hand, it is very true to say that the thing and the information will be offered to anybody as "a unit (a black box)" that it is not possible to go into further details to change, to moderate, and to manage a concerned matter. This phenomenon will likely lose a thing and information of originated matters (as many as and as much as users used to have) silently without being recognized by users.

And it also can be said that, under these situations and conditions, almost everything in the world may interfere one another randomly, massively, closely, seamlessly, dividedly without being noticed by the users. And what is more, this phenomenon will go on further beyond year by year aggressively.

In these situations, "knowledge base", "intelligent system", "AI", "Cloud", "Fog Computing", "Individual Cloud" may have played the most important role by now.

However, some researchers may have already noticed that the present "knowledge base", "intelligent system", "AI", "Cloud", "Fog Computing", "Individual Cloud" are not the ultimate AI for the human assistances. Because it is felt that there will be something lack. Namely, from the study of human behavior of the highly aged person written in this book, it is found that "a consciousness" and "a consciousness state" may role an important part in the human behavior. By putting much attention on this fact, here studies on Wet Consciousness and Dry Consciousness in the directions of novel knowledges and a creation of Dry Consciousness (Another Kind).

IMPORTANCE OF THE BOOK

There are so many kinds of tool, system, software, hardware, knowledge, thought, idea, principle, theory, and various kinds of human behaviors linked with Internetworking by Information Technologies that have been facilitating human actions even in cases at Dense Interference Space (DIS). DIS is a place where so many people or information are/is gathered randomly unintentionally on a networking or at a physical place. It will be possible to take any actions by the Interfering One Another (IOA); such as manufacturing fine goods, transporting goods, reducing a cost, solving a problem in managing a company, keeping an environment as they should be, making money, getting an information, making a new idea, learning, communicating, knowing, creating, diverging, etc. DIS could be appearing anywhere with any idea at any time purposely or coincidentally as a history tells us in the networked societies. And DIS may have an influential aspect in guiding a social and a technical direction without giving us any intention beforehand. And this tendency could not be stopped by anybody with any idea under the conventional ideas, thoughts, knowledge, and actions even though the tendency would be wanted to avoid.

In the present societies under these situations as mentioned above, there should be bearing various sorts of and many levels of DIS here and there. And some of them are brand new ones with a novel knowledge, and the others are mixed with new knowledge and conventional ones, and the another are with stuck of "obsoledge" ("obsoledge" means "obsolete" + "knowledge" by Toffler, 2010.).

Under this circumstance, any output of a service processing at DIS, for example, will be easily affected goodly or badly by Handling Method Of Knowledge (HMOK), Handling Method Of Knowledge Value (HMOKV), and Intelligence Of Knowledge (IOK) itself, which are closely related with cores of Clouds.

Technically speaking, it is now under "Techno National", "Techno Hybrid", and "Techno Global". Under these situations, industries have been transferring their production spots to abroad from a developed country to reduce a production cost and a labor cost. As result of this, some of technologies of industries in those countries should be fading away and down to nothing (zero), and what is more, a deflation will be going on in those countries. Under these situations and conditions, ordinal machines equipped industries and traditional production methods used industries may have difficult and hard moments for surviving at the places where they used to have situated at. On the other hand, it is not so easy matter to create a new industry or a company in the replaces of the conventional companies as there is not any stable space for any purpose to be achieved easily in reality.

However, at present, in terms of these matters and the phenomena that are mentioned above, it could be and can be thought of some of the methods to overcome these problems and the situations for surviving. They will be something related with "knowledge base", "intelligent system", "AI", "Cloud", "Fog Computing", "Individual Cloud". And what is more, the core matters that should be concerned will be "focusing on AI" and "putting a consciousness and a consciousness state on AI". In these meanings, senses, and aspects, this book may role a quite important part.

THE OBJECTIVE OF THE BOOK

The objective of this book are as follows:

- To share the general view of AI, an intelligent system, Cloud, etc. at present.
- To show the views of consciousness.
- To show the views of dry consciousness
- To give a necessary and important knowledge and information for undergraduate, graduate, Doctor candidate, post doctor in order to extend their ideas into further beyond. And hopefully to bring their ideas and thoughts into reality.

THE CHALLENGES

Strictly speaking, the challenges are as follows;

- To show the necessary and important points of the next step for AI.
- To show the view of consciousness.
- To show the consciousness pictures and mechanisms for Wet Consciousness and Dry Consciousness (Another Kind).

AUDIENCE

Important audiences are researchers and engineers in computer science, AI, AI application areas, intelligent robotics, intelligent systems, Cloud, Fog Computing, Individual Cloud, and related.

In addition, undergraduate and graduate students in computer science, control, AI, robotics, Cloud, operations research, information, and intelligent systems studies are recommended to read. For under graduate students, from Chapter 1 to Chapter 4 will be recommended to read. And for graduate students, from Chapter 5 to Chapter 10 will be recommended to read.

In addition, post graduate students and researchers in computer science, control, AI, robotics, Cloud, operations research, information, and intelligent systems studies are also recommended to read. And for post graduate students and researchers, from Chapter 8 to Chapter 11 will be recommended to read.

The intended audiences are researchers in different fields seeking for brand new disciplines. And researchers in different application fields are also intended for them to get new concepts through this book. And other fields of engineers are also intended for assisting their systems to level-up.

ORGANIZATION OF THE BOOK

The book is organized by 11 chapters. A brief description of each of the chapters are as follows:

Chapter 1 Is "AI in General"

There are many kinds of Artificial Intelligence (AI) usages in almost every field. AI is quite often used for control, Computer Aided Design and Computer Aided Manufacturing (CAD/CAM), machine control, Computer Integrated Manufacturing (CIM), production spot control, factory control, intelligent control, intelligent system, deep learning, Cloud, knowledge base, data base, management, production system, statistics, sales force, environment examination, agriculture, art, livings, daily life, etc. Those usages are helpful, useful, and reliable. Because the outputs come up to us soon after commands are input by manual or by voice. And the output results will be used for practical usages of jobs, daily life, entertainment, research, and many others. Under these situations, the present AI usages will be reexamined whether there is any matter to be considered further or not in AI research directions and their purposes behind by looking at the history of AI developments.

Chapter 2 Is "Consciousness in General"

Consciousness studies have nowadays become a general and an open question in the research areas. As the result of this situation, there are many research papers on this subject. Under this situation, it is worthwhile considering a present direction and a reason of those studies in order to find out a next direction and the reason for the further research. And then, from those the direction and the reason, try to find out a necessity and a reason for the further research step. By doing these things, here also talks and shows about "Consciousness in General" in a sense of functional mechanisms both at the past and the present.

Chapter 3 Is "General Activities of Brain as Function"

Most of the living creatures have Accumulated Neuron Processing Unit Area (ANPUA) in their bodies. Most of them are placed and centered at brain in a head for processing various kinds of human related information. They behave like a central processing unit (CPU) in a digital computer system from a point of functional view. Here talks about general activities of brain as a point of functional behavior. And talks about a digital computer from the same functional point of view. And then talks and argues about the differences between a brain (Wet Brain) and a digital computer (Dry Brain) whether there is any or not. If there is any difference, the difference will be deepened for further studies in order to find out the major functions of general activities of brain.

Chapter 4 Is "Wet Consciousness and Dry Consciousness"

In this chapter, Wet Consciousness and Dry Consciousness will be defined. For doing the definitions, firstly here talks about the differences between Wet Consciousness and Dry Consciousness under the understandings at present. Wet Consciousness is a living creature brain and Dry Consciousness is an entity made by a digital computer, so called. Naturally, consciousness itself is also argued on what it is and on its general understanding of mechanisms. And then talk and argue about the Wet Consciousness mechanisms. And the possibility to create Dry Consciousness will be studied under these situations.

Chapter 5 Is "Case of a Person on Consciousness Level"

Here talks about the consciousness studies through Caring For (attending-to) Highly Aged Person (CFHAP). And talks about the novel knowledges obtained through CFHAP on brain activities related matters of a cerebrum and a cerebellum.

Through a highly aged person's attending-to, it happened coincidentally to notice the curious brain behaviors in the "from-awake-to-sleep process". They might be related with a consciousness state, mind, intention, attention, perception, recognition, understanding, and action. From these behaviors, it might be also possible to understand some of the brain mechanisms in a consciousness state and a mind state.

In these regards, this chapter will show the patient symptoms, the bodily movements, and the behaviors.

Chapter 6 Is "Human Behavior as First Person"

Here tries to talk about First Person known as the grammatical person (first person, second person, third person) basically and then the talk goes to a theoretical argument of First Person in a frame work of brain activities (cerebrum, cerebellum) as they are known and understood now. And then, the arguments will go to a practical argument by using the novel knowledges as shown in the chapter 5. In this way, it will be further studied and will be more deepened in order to get the general basic brain functions of First Person. They will be described as a notion on First Person.

Some part of the previous Chapter will be repeated for the arguments to go smoothly.

Chapter 7 is "Human Behavior as Second Person"

Here tries to talk about Second Person known as the grammatical person (first person, second person, third person) basically and then the talk goes to a theoretical argument of Second Person in a frame work of brain activities (cerebrum, cerebellum) as they are known and understood now. And then, the arguments will go to a practical argument by using the novel knowledges as shown in the chapter 5. In this way, it will be further studied and will be more deepened in order to get the general basic brain functions of Second Person. They will be described as a notion on Second Person.

Some part of the previous Chapter will be repeated for the arguments to go smoothly.

Chapter 8 Is "Another Kind as First Person"

Here talks about First Person as an artificial entity. Firstly, First Person will be defined by using the notions in Chapter 6 and chapter 7. And the functions of First Person will be argued and studied as a point of views of the mechanisms. Secondly, the functions of First Person will be transformed into a computer system by using a rough modal method (not The Fourier Modal Method). This method is simply to replace a function of First Person that is discovered as described in Chapter 6 and Chapter 7 into a modal function of a computer system as an artificial entity.

Some part of the previous Chapters will be repeated for the arguments to go smoothly.

Chapter 9 Is "Another Kind as Second Person"

Here talks about Second Person as an artificial entity. Firstly, Second Person will be defined by using the notions in Chapter 6 and chapter 7. And the functions of Second Person will be argued and studied as a point of views of the mechanisms. Secondly, the functions of Second Person will be transformed into a computer system by using a rough modal method (not The Fourier Modal Method). This method is simply to replace a function of Second Person that is discovered as described in Chapter 6 and Chapter 7 into a modal function of a computer system as an artificial entity.

Some part of the previous Chapters will be repeated for the arguments to go smoothly.

Chapter 10 Is "Another Kind in Consciousness"

Here talks about an artificial entity which may have a consciousness state. The ideas of First Person and Second Person in this book chapters will be cored and used basically for an implementation of the entity. Firstly, a general description of the entity will be argued and discussed again by using the notions in the chapter 6 and the chapter 7. And then the general structure of the entity will be roughly shown by using RMM and the notions from the chapter 6, the chapter 7, the chapter 8, and the chapter 9. And then, secondly the simplest example by using the entity will be given by RMM. And the finally, it will be evaluated.

Some part of the previous Chapters will be repeated for the arguments to go smoothly.

Chapter 11 Is "Future Works"

All over the Chapters will be concluded in the directions of the future works in general. And some of the important factors for the further studies will be extracted and argued on the views of mechanisms and connections. And also some of the important augmented groups of neurons will be picked up and will be talked about the future studies especially on brand new functions and mechanisms. And also as the related matters, some of the concepts (for example; good, bad, Like, Dislike, Love, Affection, Reflection, etc.) will be talked about for the further studies. And finally, all about the human brain will be wrap up for further studies.

REFERENCES

Sugiyama, S. (2008). Fundamental Behavior. In *Communication Method*. Beijing, China: IEEE/SOLI.

Sugiyama, S. (2013). *Intangible Capital Management Method As Dynamic Knowledge Wisdom. In Intellectual Capital Management For Knowledge-Based Organizations*. Hershey, PA: IGI Global.

Sugiyama, S., & Suzuki, J. (2012). *Accumulation and Integration in Seamless Knowledge. International Journal of Asian Business and Information Management*.

Toffler & Toffler. (2010). *40 for the next 40*. Toffler Associates. Retrieved October, 2010, from www.htmq.com/mirai/next40.shtml

Acknowledgment

This book is dedicated to my mother:

First of all, I would like to give great and warm thanks to my mother. Because I have got some knowledge about consciousness, first person, and second person mechanisms of a brain through "24 Hours Attending-To My Mother for Two Years" in the six years' Caring-For. So, I would like to share the happiness of this achievement of the book publishing mostly with my mother.

Secondly, I would like to also give great thanks and appreciation to IGI Global for having given me this opportunity of book publication as IGI Global has been advising and assisting me all through the publication processes.

Chapter 1
Artificial Intelligence in General

ABSTRACT

There are many kinds of uses for artificial intelligence (AI) in almost every field. AI is quite often used for control, computer aided design (CAD) and computer aided manufacturing (CAM), machine control, computer integrated manufacturing (CIM), production spot control, factory control, intelligent control, intelligent systems, deep learning, the cloud, knowledge bases, database, management, production systems, statistics, to assist sales forces, environment examination, agriculture, art, livings, daily life, etc. The present AI uses will be reexamined whether there is any matter to be considered further or not in AI research directions and their purposes behind the current status by looking at the history of AI development.

INTRODUCTION

Nowadays, there are so many huge, complex, chaotic systems, with tremendous huge data archives, individual but directly to the accumulated database, huge image data archives, research paper databases, accumulated individual archives (document and image), randomly accumulated data archives, etc. There are so many kinds of matters and so many sorts of data around us. Indeed, it is not possible to handle these situations properly in order to get intended answers without any kind of AI usage.

DOI: 10.4018/978-1-5225-8217-5.ch001

Here, first, AI history will be looked back upon by starting with control in general. Second, knowledge systems will be looked at. Third, present AI usage will be discussed compared to the situations of today.

BACKGROUND

Control in General

In the past, the first significant work in automatic control was James Watt's centrifugal governor for the speed control of a steam engine in order to control the vapor pressure of the tank in 1788, in England. From this invention, there were various kinds of studies on controls. During the decade of the 1940's, the frequency-response method made it possible for engineers to design linear feedback control systems that satisfied performance requirements. From the end of the 1940's to early 1950's, the root-locus method in control system design was fully developed. These methods are the essence of the classical control. Because of the system to treat many inputs and outputs, these methods became less significant. As the result of this, the modern control theories had been developed from around 1960's. In the modern control theories, linear control method, non-linear control method, and discrete control method have been developed by the help of computer more and more in the directions of deterministic and stochastic systems, the adaptive system, and learning control of complex systems.

The applications of modern control theories had been expanding quite rapidly to geology, economics, medicine, and sociology. Moreover, with the developing of the micro processors' process speeds and those kinds of software, it has become possible to have a discrete control and to have expert systems which are able to mimic human skills in manufacturing and in thought of thinking.

Almost in the same period, petri net, neural network, fuzzy logic, genetic algorithm, immune control method, chaos, complexity, and the others have come up to the world as intelligent control methods. Indeed, they were tried to use in complex and huge systems.

Production Control in Past, Present, and Future

Especially in these forty years, the production systems and their control methods have been changed drastically. The assisted parts in production have been shifted from power to human knowledge as shown below.

1. **Use of Mechanical Power:** This is the primitive stage of human assisted method. The assisted parts are power of rotation, forward movement, and backward movement. Those other simply assisted movements are used.
2. **Assistance of Skill:** Some processing skills of methods in productions are assisted by computer systems. This assistance includes a craft work.
3. **Replace a Part of Skill:** Some processing skills of methods in productions are replaced by computer systems (knowledge base). This replacement includes a craft work.
4. **Replace a Part of Job at Present:** Some processing parts of job in productions are replaced by computer systems (intelligent control, AI, or intelligent system). This replacement includes a craft work.
5. **Replace a Job at Present:** Some jobs in productions are replaced by computer systems (AI, or intelligent system). This replacement includes a craft job working.
6. **Assistance of Human Thinking at Present:** Some human thinking is assisted by computer systems (AI, or cloud). This replacement includes a craft job working.
7. **Assistance of Human in Future:** Human is assisted by computer systems (AI, cloud, mini cloud, individual cloud, consciousness, or another kind).

These phenomena are also observed by the facilities and the systems in Production Control that have been used today as shown below.

1. Exclusive use of computer assisted machine
2. Group controlled machine system
3. Automatic machine
4. Computer Integrated Manufacturing (CIM)
5. Process control by genetic algorithm, fuzzy logic, and neural networking
6. Total control system

7. Knowledge base
8. Management system in complexity
9. Knowledge base and AI
10. AI and cloud in future
11. AI, cloud, and consciousness in future

Through observing these developments in production control, it is obvious that many kinds of production and management systems and facilities including computer have been developed in order to assist a manager and a worker physically in an effective way. Now, it is a small and a tiny phenomenon. However, a human assisted system by using a knowledge base, AI, cloud, and consciousness is beginning to come up for real usages in the near future.

Production Control Problems in Knowledge Systems

The general phenomenon is shown and described and some major difficulties on production control in knowledge systems are discussed.

1. **Agile Production:** The most important thing for the industries to be existed is to offer desired production goods on the time wanted with the highest quality and the necessary quantity, whose conditions should be followed by efficient and effective ways. This is the only way to satisfy the needs in the society.

There are many kinds of facilities and many kinds of production knowledge systems which can facilitate a production quite easily. However, there are still the cost matters left. In another words, if a good system is invented, there must be soon some ones who are going to use the same kind of the system in somewhere at the same time in the world. As the result of this, CEOs of companies have been always facing this kind of the problem (Agile Production) which cannot be ignored. On the other hand, it should take a lot of time to invent and to develop a new effective production knowledge system.

2. **Huge and Complex System:** In order to improve productivity and efficiency in a total management, the control area should have been expanded more and more from a tiny spot of a machine to a whole company. As the result of this, the system to be treated has become so huge and complex. After all, the conventional knowledge system methods have become less effective for getting the profits.

4

3. **Networking Allover:** In production and in sales, the globalization has come up in many decades ago, so the functions of a company have been distributed various places physically in all over the world. But those places always need very intimate and close relationships one another in order to create the most profitable output. As the result of this, they need to behave as if they are very close and near physically. Namely, it is very important to behave as if they are one unit by networking allover.

4. **Intelligence Like Human:** It is quite important to watch the knowledge system closely whether it goes well or goes wrong even though the knowledge system is controlled automatically. Since the knowledge system easily will go wrong to disturbances. In order to get it back to the normal situation, it needs proficiency of human to do it. However, to reduce this burden, the knowledge system needs a kind of intelligence to do automatically instead of human.

Production Control Method and Difficulty

How today's methods including the conventional methods worked and are working in order to reduce the problems mentioned is examined. Also, if today's methods do not work well, it shows what sort of difficulties that they are facing.

Conventional Method

For controlling a motor, air or oil flow, etc., there is a method of continuous control method. In this method, the behavior of a whole system must be written mathematically in detail. This phenomenon made the control area transfer into a special field. If it is failed to express a target system mathematically in detail, a lot of optimizations must be done. As the result of this, it may lose the accuracy in control.

There are types of control methods, which are an open-loop control system and a closed-loop control system. The open-loop control system is the control action is not influenced by the results of that action. Some desired or reference input is sensed and amplified and then operated upon by the controller. The controller uses an external power source to apply the proper control action to the system being controlled. The output is strictly influenced by the input value, by the precision of the amplifier, and by the controller that are expected to have no noise from the outside for the system operation. Hence for each reference input, there corresponds a fixed operating condition. Namely, the accuracy of the system is dependent upon the calibration. This control method has a difficulty in that the open-loop control system can be used in practice only if the relationship between the input and output is known, only if there the relationship between the input and output is known, and only if there are neither internal nor external disturbances.

The closed-loop control system is the output quantity is feedback for comparison with the input. Also, the difference or the error quantity is then applied to the amplifier in order to reduce the error and bring the output of the system to a desired value. This is superior to the open-loop control system in the accuracy and this is more robust in the disturbance which might be appeared to the system. This system is mathematically expressed by Input [I], Transfer Function [T], and Output [O]. In addition, the target system of the whole needs to be defined mathematically with continuous functions (linear or non-linear functions). However, even if the target system is quite large, it should be clearly defined mathematically all through the system. Once the system has been defined, it should keep the system structure as it was (whatever happens to the system). Variable numbers to the input are limited to under certain numbers. Namely, it is not allowed to put any number of variables needed as an input function. As the results of these, the following difficulties will come up.

1. It is hard to apply these methods in excessively complex and huge system.
2. It is quite hard to use irrational function.
3. It is impossible to use graphically and experimentally expressed data.
4. It is hard to put intelligence into the control system.
5. It is quite hard to modify the system to the continuous change of the condition.

Another Method

1. **Discrete Control Method:** Discrete-time systems, or sampled-data systems, are dynamic systems in which one or more variables can be changed only at discrete instants of time. These instants may specify the time at which some physical measurement is performed or the time at which the memory of a digital computer is read out, etc. The time interval between two discrete instants is taken to be sufficiently short so that the data for the time between these discrete instants can be approximated by a simple interpolation. Discrete-time systems differ

from continuous-time ones in that the signals for a discrete-time are in sampled-data form. The basic idea is almost the same as the methods mentioned above, but only the mathematical expression is different. Namely, this system is mathematically expressed by Input [I]*, Transfer Function [T]*, and Output [O]*. Some of the advantages of digital controllers and analogue controllers may be summarized as follows:

a. Digital controllers (computers) are capable of perform complex computations with constant accuracy at a high speed. Digital computers can have almost any desired degree of accuracy in computations at relatively little increase in cost.

b. Digital controllers make use of larger systems compared with the analogue controllers.

c. Digital controllers are extremely versatile. By merely issuing a new program, one can completely change the operations being performed. This feature is particularly important if the control system is to receive operating information or instructions from the manager of the company, where the total company analysis and optimization studies are being made.

So as the results of these, this method is better off than the conventional methods in a sense of treatment in the system operation.

2. **Group Control Method:** Group control method has made the physical world to control from one object to group of objects. The objects are networked together by RS232C series terminals one by one in the very early stage. The system contains the central network control terminal at which all information goes out and goes in with necessary information. The network information is encapsulated as a packet and is sent out to terminals from one by one. This method could reduce the time to bring information to each terminal of the whole system physically. It has become soon fossil because factory was forced to produce many kinds of items with only one production line at the same time.

Production Control Problems in AI

AI is a growing field that covers many disciplines. Also, there are many ways to define the field of AI. As a science, essentially as part of cognitive science, the goal of AI is to understand principles that makes intelligence possible. As a technology and as a part of computer science, the goal of AI is to design an intelligent computer system that exhibits the characteristics associated with intelligence in human behavior; i.e., understanding language and picture, learning, reasoning, solving problems, and so on. Specializations in AI include knowledge representations, problem solving, learning, natural language understanding, computer vision, robotics, AI language, expert systems, and several others. Many of these areas related to each other. Here describes a little bit more in detail about the typical areas of researches.

1. **Natural Language:** Automated natural language understanding has been major research area since the earliest days of AI. Understanding natural language involves three levels of interpretation: syntactic, semantic, and pragmatic levels.

Syntactic processes "parse" sentences to make the grammatical relationships between words in sentences clear. Semantics is concerned with assigning meaning to one another and to the surrounding context. The boundaries separating these levels are not distinct. Particularly, sentences need not pass through these levels of interpretation sequentially. Research continues into how to integrate information from any level when it is needed.

2. **Computer Vision:** The basic objective of computer vision research is to interpret pictures. What "interpreting pictures" means differs depending upon the application to which the interpretation is to be put in. For example, in interpreting satellite images it may be sufficient to roughly identify regions of forest blight or crop damage. Robot vision systems may find it necessary to precisely identify assembly components to accurately affix the components to the part under assembly. And another example of study is; extracted image in a scene of town, street, houses, people, etc. will be processed by a computer in order to assist human behavior of management, data retrieving, etc.

3. **Expert System:** Expert systems are computer programs whose behavior duplicates, in some sense, the abilities of a human exert in his/her area of expertise. There are many examples of such programs from the fabled system which performs automatic analysis of chemical spectroscopes through various medical systems such as the drug prescribes and the diagnosis program to the geological prospector.

While any design methodology can be used to build an expert system, the majority of these systems are implemented in production system architectures. A production system is an ordered set of "if-then" or pattern-action rules whose action part is executed when the pattern part matches incoming data or data retrieved from previous rule execution.

4. **Theorem Proving and Logic Programming:** Theorem proving refers to the process of making logical deductions starting from a non-contradictory set of axioms specified in predicate calculus. Robinson (1996) showed how it was possible to totally automate this process using a method called "resolution". The resolution principle underlies almost all theorem-proving research.

Any assertion that is to be proved using resolution theorem-proving techniques is first represented as a formula in the predicated calculus and then its negation is added to the set of axioms. A purely mechanical set of transformations can then be carried out by the theorem-proving program to put the axioms and negated assertion into so-called clause form. Any pair of these clauses can be "resolved" against one another in a matching process that results in the creation of a third clause that logically follows from the previous two clauses. The resolution method automatically performs series of such resolutions, eventually building tree of clause, resolvents, resolvents of resolvents, and so on. If eventually two clauses resolve to nil, then the two clauses are contradiction which, in turn, implies. Finally, that the assertion has been proved since its negation caused a non-contradictory set off clauses to become contradictory.

5. **Knowledge Represented:** For a system to be able to behave intelligently it must have knowledge of its domain of expertise. This knowledge includes facts and rules for manipulating these facts. Over the years, numbers of different knowledge representations "paradigms" have emerged. One of the earliest such schemes represented knowledge in semantic networks where facts are stored at nodes, and relationships between the facts are represented by arcs. One of the most common relationships in semantic networks is the omni-present ISA link which allows facts to be attached to classes of objects and then inherited by specific objects in the class.

6. **Learning:** Learning had not been a major concern for AI. Most AI researchers seemed to have felt that it was first necessary to concentrate on how to make a program do something before figuring out how it could learn to do it. Still, a small cadre of "learning aficionados" had been attempting to explore the basic issues in learning, and learning has begun to take on ever increasing significance in AI.

7. **Dynamic Knowledge Base:** This is simply to make an artifact like a certain kind of human knowledge which is able to understand the matter, knowledge, and figure. This is being done with various methods. For example, S. Sugiyama is introduced that some kinds of human knowledge are able to be represented and be stored into a computer system by using the back propagation neural networks (BPNN). Moreover, he showed that these kinds of the knowledge include remembering, retrieving, deducing, and some kind of logical thinking-out can be done (Sugiyama, 1996). However, the abilities achieved by those methods are quite different from the human knowledge which is able to think-out dynamically as our human does. But this is the main and the most important issue for getting the mechanisms of AI by using a computer. So, it can be said that this will be the one of the key fields in AI studies.

8. **Consciousness:** This topic is now becoming the most important and growing field in various fields of science studies. In fact, the European Neural Network Society, IEEE, SPIE, and other major societies in these related fields open an academic research on the problem of consciousness in their interests. One of the prominent institutes in this study is in Arizona University. They have got their own institute especially on this study. Indeed, they offer several courses in study like MS, PhD, etc.

Main reasons for this study are focused into three points:

a. In order to address the problem of consciousness at a higher level.
b. In order to relax a certain type of academic taboo.
c. In order to get an extended knowledge out of this field in order to apply it to other fields of studies like a neural network, an artificial intelligence, various fields of control, a soft computing, etc.

9. **Distributed Computing Method:** Distributed computing creates the foundation for manufacturing mediated via intranet of the Internet. In its simplest form, distributed computing is having two or more computers connected by a network that is working to solve the same problem. Real manufacturing is more complicated, i.e., the machines and the

computers implemented a factory should be coordinated/collaborated with one another. The coordination/collaboration pattern is not unique, but it depends on the type of manufacturing and a company. So usually it is very hard to manage the whole system. However, the Internet and intranets are used for getting them work together.

10. **Agent Method:** The Agents are intelligent software programs that can travel through intranets or the Internet to gather information on purchasing, design, production, planning, resources, and other factors in manufacturing supply chain, and to bring together all parts of the process at the appropriate time. Different types of agents specialize in different components of manufacturing. For example, some seek design data, and others deal with scheduling and planning. Agent-based approaches can optimize manufacturing in several ways, from increasing enterprises' responsiveness to the market's requirements to allocating resources most effectively to increase the effectiveness of information exchange and feedback. But it is hard to make a proper agent which is able to satisfy the demands. It is also hard to have a necessary information exchange method among the agents.

11. **Holonic Method:** The word "Holon" is firstly used in the book called "The Ghost in the Machine", London, 1976 by Arthur Koestler. He introduced the idea of "Self-regulating Open Hierarchic Order (SOHO)". This idea has become a current issue in study of a control field. In Europe this is developed and studied in some decades ago, but mainly only the idea of "Holon" is philosophically taken and the model behaves holonically (with the idea of "Holon") under only a few conditions. In Australia, US, and Japan, the situation is almost the same as Europe.

By using the idea of Holon, a huge and complex system can be expressed by the holarchy and this idea can be applied to an engineering control field. However, this idea is still in need of a mathematical investigation and study in order to treat it logically and systematically.

12. **System Management Method in Complexity:** The phenomenon of Chaos is found and studied first by the emeritus professor Y. Ueda at Kyoto University in 1967 and L. York defied it theoretically (Li et al, 1875) In 1987, Chaos by James Gleick became a best seller in 1987. Since then, this world seemed to be caught up by this idea. And many kinds of the phenomenon in this world have been explained, expressed, or described by this idea. Since then, mathematical explanations have

been given to this idea, but it is still under-going theme to solve as Dr. S. Daw who is a researcher at the Oak Ridge National Laboratory in Oak Ridge said at the fifth annual conference on Chaos in Manufacturing in Santa Fe, N.M., April, 1997;

...No one can yet define complexity or say exactly how to manage a company in accordance with its principles. But computer tools exist to predict explosions and metal fatigue where once the timing of such a failure was anybody's guess.

Now there is the general algorithm (the typical steps) by J. Gleick in building a simulation model of Chaos.

Step 1: Simplify the problem as much as possible what is essential.

Step 2: Write program which simulates many components following simple rules with specified interactions and randomizing elements.

Step 3: Run program many times with different random number seeds, collecting data and statistics from the different runs.

Step 4: Attempt to understand how the simple rules gave rise to the observed behavior.

Step 5: Perform parameter changes and "legions" on the program to locate the sources of behavior and the effects of different parameters.

Step 6: Simplify the simulation even further if possible. Or add additional elements that were found to be a necessary.

But this idea is still in need of a mathematical investigation and study in order to treat it logically and systematically.

MAIN FOCUS OF THE CHAPTER

AI at Present

AI in a broad sense has started as a control method of objects, machines, and production systems in order to help or to replace human skills from centuries ago. Since then, as the concept of AI itself has been studied, developed, and expanded by researchers and engineers, the target objects have also been broadened widely and deeply from a simple machine to a complex system and from a management of company to a human assist. In addition, in these years AI has come to the initial space pint that is able to assist and to replace core human related matters of thoughts by AI itself. Those kinds of typical phenomenon are cloud, big data, and deep learning.

Cloud at Present

The word of "cloud" has come to this world many decades ago from workstation computer company researcher. The time has passed for some decades without being paid any attention by researchers and engineers in the world. But the end of 20th century, "cloud" comes up to this world suddenly again without any notice. Cloud related hardware and software have been fulfilled so much and so many in this world. But they are not friendly to users at all at the first stage because the systems and the many kinds of software are not user friendly at all at the first stage. They seemed only to give software wanted to user platform remotely and there are any data shares for the software. However, as the first stage, cloud gave a good and nice impression to most of the users. Some of them are as follows:

1. **SAP:** Systems Applications Products (ERP- Enterprise Resource Planning)
2. **SOA:** Service Oriented Architecture
3. **SaaS:** Software as a Service
4. **Mash Up:** Mashing up software
5. **Meta Frame:** Peer to peer relation
6. **PaaS:** Platform as a Service
7. **HaaS:** Hardware as a Service
8. **IaaS:** Infrastructure as a Service
9. **Cloud:** Cloud computing within a specific area
10. **Mini Cloud:** Various kinds of small cloud

Those systems and functions mentioned above may have been concluded as part of cloud computing in order to solve problems at company.

Nowadays, cloud has become more users friendly. Moreover, broad ways of usages have been offered from cloud to desktop, laptop, and smart phone.

The cloud may have an ability to offer and to assist any kind of useful information without any limitations for users. However, it does not go straightly to the space of cloud mentioned above at present. The reason why it is so is that there must be something missing for the AI that the present cloud possesses.

Of course, there have come out of fog computing, mini cloud, and individual cloud in order to assist and help human behaviors (desires, wants, actions, thoughts, think-out, intentions, attentions).

However, those ideas mentioned above will not have given any feelings to be able to replace human behaviors.

Big Data and Deep Learning at Present

In this world, there are full of data that have been produced by individuals, machines, systems, and all human related matters. This tendency has been growing time by time and moment by moment, which makes the data in this world truly big data. In these situations, big data and deep learning has come up to the research spaces and the application fields such as image processing, computer vision, speech recognition, natural language processing, audio recognition, social network filtering, machine translation, bioinformatics, relation search, logistics, various geological data processing, and drug design.

Under such big data and deep learning situations, "deep learning" is explained by researchers and Wikipedia as follows.

Uthra Kunathur Thikshaja and Anand Paul present deep learning as (Thikshaja et al, 2018).

Deep learning is a branch of machine learning based on a set of algorithms that can be used to model high-level abstractions in data by using multiple processing layers with complex structure, or otherwise composed of multiple non-linear transformation

Wikipedia presents deep learning as ("Deep Learning", n.d.).

Most modern deep learning models are based on an artificial neural network although they can also include propositional formulas or latent variables organized layer-wise in deep generative models such as the nodes in Deep Belief Networks and Deep Boltzmann Machines.

In deep learning, each level learns to transform its input data into a slightly more abstract and composite representation. In an image recognition application, the raw input may be a matrix of pixels; the first representational layer may abstract the pixels and encode edges; the second layer may compose and encode arrangements of edges; the third layer may encode a nose and eyes; and the fourth layer may recognize that the image contains a face. Importantly, a deep learning process can learn which features to optimally place in which level on its own. (Of course, this does not completely obviate the need for hand-tuning; for example, varying numbers of layers and layer sizes can provide different degrees of abstraction.)

The "deep" in "deep learning" refers to the number of layers through which the data is transformed. More precisely, deep learning systems have a substantial credit assignment path (CAP) depth. The CAP is the chain of transformations from input to output. CAPs describe potentially causal connections between input and output. For a feedforward neural network, the depth of the CAPs is that of the network and is the number of hidden layers plus one (as the output layer is also parameterized). For recurrent neural networks, in which a signal may propagate through a layer more than once, the CAP depth is potentially unlimited. No universally agreed upon threshold of depth divides shallow learning from deep learning, but most researchers agree that deep learning involves CAP depth > 2. CAP of depth 2 has been shown to be a universal approximator in the sense that it can emulate any function. Beyond that more layers do not add to the function approximator ability of the network. The extra layers help in learning features."

CONCLUSION

AI has been shown and discussed in this chapter from the beginning of initial thought with historical aspect. Also, as the present situation, cloud and deep learning with big data have been shown.

From the development point of view, the following things can be summarized:

1. AI is a quite useful tool for a human assistance, but it is still under development.
2. The idea of cloud and deep learning with big data is not enough to assist and replace human activities at the moment.
3. Cloud and deep learning are naturally not conscious about what they are doing by themselves. So what they are doing is simply like "action with careless", which is different from human.
4. AI needs more space for assisting and replacing human activities.

REFERENCES

Li, T. Y., & Yorke, J. A. (1875). Periodic Three Implies Chaos. *The American Mathematical Monthly*, *82*(10), 985–992. doi:10.1080/00029890.1975.11994008

Robinson, J. A. (1996). *A machine oriented logic based on the resolution principle*. Association for Computing Machinery.

Sugiyama, S. (1996). Knowledge Processor. *Paper presented at the conference of International Conference on Information Systems Analysis and Synthesis*.

Sugiyama, S. (2001). *Virtual-Space Factory: General Concept of Holonic Control*. Unpublished doctoral dissertation, University of Gifu, Gifu, Japan.

Thikshaja, U. K., & Paul, A. (2018). A Brief Review on Deep Learning and Types of Implementation for Deep Learning. In Deep Learning Innovations and Their Convergence With Big Data (pp. 20-32). Hershey, PA: IGI Global. doi:10.4018/978-1-5225-3015-2.ch002

Wikipedia. (n.d.). *Deep Learning*. Retrieved from en.wikipedia.org/wiki/Deep_learning

KEY TERMS AND DEFINITIONS

AI: Artificial Intelligence. It is same field of Machine Learning.

Cloud: It has the ability to offer and to assist any kind of useful information without any limitations for users.

Deep Learning: It is a branch of machine learning based on a set of algorithms that can be used to model high-level abstractions in data by using multiple processing layers with complex structure, or otherwise composed of multiple non-linear transformations.

Dynamic Knowledge Base: It is simply to make an artifact like a certain kind of human knowledge which is able to understand matter, knowledge, and figure.

OA: Service Oriented Planning.

SAP: Systems Applications Products (ERP- Enterprise Resource Planning).

Chapter 2
Consciousness in General

ABSTRACT

Consciousness studies have nowadays become a general and an open question in the research areas. As the result of this situation, there are many research papers on this topic. Under this situation, it is worthwhile considering a present direction and a reason of those studies in order to find out a next direction and the reason for the further research. Then, from those the direction and the reason, try to find out a necessity and a reason for the further research step. This chapter presents consciousness in general in a sense of functional mechanisms both at the past and at the present.

INTRODUCTION

In chapter 1, AI in general has been considered and argued under the points of historical background, historical development, various kinds of AI methods in the past, and recent AI methods. However, it seems that, these methods cannot escape from the limitations of usages, small human replacement possibilities, and an increment of processing knowledge unless otherwise a completely new idea is originated and implemented. This chapter provides the differences between the present AI and human brain in a sense of the processing methods. The complete differences of AI and human brain are presented as following:

DOI: 10.4018/978-1-5225-8217-5.ch002

1. AI at present is very good at high processing speed within a limited subject (image, relation search, geological processing, etc.). However, human brain is slower than AI in a processing speed.
2. Human brain has an ability to solve a new problem by doing the processes intension, attention, recognition, think, think-out (solve problem), and behavior (action) under a consciousness state. However, deep learning does not have the same kinds of processes.
3. AI is theoretically scalable in data search, but human has the limitations.
4. AI and human brain do some kinds of abstraction in data/information processing at each process, but the methods that they use are different from each other.
5. AI itself does not have any thought of mind (consciousness) for any processing, but human brain does.

This complete difference simply shows that there are differences between the present AI and human brain in their functions and their behaviors. So firstly, the meaning of these differences will be discussed and considered. Secondly, the present understanding of consciousness is shown by using Wikipedia and two understandings papers. Those will be done in the next section background and try to find out the present direction and the reason about what brain (consciousness) is.

BACKGROUND

The differences of AI and human brain are as the following:

1. AI at present is very good at high processing speed within a limited subject (image, relation search, geological processing, etc.). However, human brain is slower than AI in a processing speed.

Now, AI can detect a human movement and a face figure very fast compared with human brain. It is used for security reasons at all over places in the real world. AI can do all over detections of a target object, like tall or small?, man or woman?, young or old?, wear hat?, with glasses?, and with bag in arm as simple functions.

However, human brain can do detailed detections like the height is a bit small, the walking rhythm is a bit fast, and the clothes to wear are not the usual ones. These things are only able to be done under a consciousness state with the five senses by human brain. Since a detailed thing to detect is necessary to watch from many aspects, like movement, speed, sound, behavior, rhythm, figure, impression, etc. under those association processes at the same moment.

2. Human brain has an ability to solve a new problem by doing the processes intension, attention, recognition, think, think-out (solve problem), and behavior (action) under a consciousness state. But deep learning does not take the same kinds of the processes of human brain.

Now, AI can do things with some kinds of abstraction such as raw data to first processed data, next processed data, etc. at each step of the process in order to get the final output desired. These abstraction processes taken by AI are always the same. As the result of this phenomenon, it may be said that deep learning has a rigid and a limited processing mechanism. Therefore, the output desired is always the same whatever happens to AI surroundings.

However, human brain does things under a consciousness state at each step such as intension, attention, recognition, think, think-out, and behavior in order to get the final output desired. Human brain does also abstractions of the processing information at each step, but they are not the same as AI. The final output of human brain desire might be different from at each process if the consciousness state is different from at each process.

3. AI is theoretically scalable in data and information searches, but human brain has the limitations.

Now, AI can do data and information searches without limitations, theoretically. It is just a matter of the processing time.

However, human brain actually has certain limit for processing data and information. Data and information searches in the reflection processes of human brain will be done and performed within a limited area of human brain. In this sense, human brain itself is not scalable for processing data and information as a function.

4. AI and human brain do some kinds of abstraction in data or information processing at each process, but the methods that they use are different from each other.

Now, human brain does some kinds of abstraction in data or information processing. It will be done by image reflection process, listening reflection process, or any other reflection process in a consciousness state. More in detail, human brain does abstraction under a consciousness state at each step in order to get the final output desired.

However, AI does some kinds of abstraction in data or information processing within a limited space. In addition, an abstraction processes taken by AI is always the same.

5. AI itself does not have any thought of mind (consciousness) for any processing, but human does.

Now, AI does not have mind, so called, for any processing. The processing is done by sequentially one code by one code in order, so that there is not any room for the mind state that affects to the processing result even if AI were to have mind. However, human does have mind with five senses as we feel.

Brain at Present

Science alert (Business Insider) introduces the following things about human brain from the recent studies.

1. **There Are 'Left Brain' and 'Right Brain' People:** No scientific studies have really ever been able to prove that people are dominated by either side of the brain.
2. **We Only Use 10% of Our Brain:** In fact, we use pretty much all of our brain – studies have shown how our brains are engaged in even the smallest cursory tasks.
3. **We All Have a 'Learning Style':** Many people were taught that they had a "learning style" at school. The idea comes from that some people are better at retaining information orally, visually, or by listening. But there is actually very little scientific evidence that the learning styles exist.
4. **It's All Downhill When You Turn 40:** Some cognitive skills do decline as you get older. But new research recently found that older people experience more "tip of the tongue" moments too, which is where you know the word you want, but your brain can't quite get to it. But getting older does have some brain benefits.

5. **Men and Women Learn Differently:** Ultimately, we don't know enough about the brain to draw any meaningful conclusions about how men and women learn.
6. **There Are Only 5 Senses:** We are taught early on at school about the five senses: sight, hearing, taste, smell, and touch. But it's actually more complicated than that, and we have a few more. Some neuroscientists list up to 21 slightly different ways of sensing things.
7. **Drinking Alcohol Kills Your Brain Cells:** Too much alcohol can make us slur and fall around, so it's not an uncommon assumption that it hurts our brain cells.
8. **Brain Damage Is Permanent:** The brain is what controls everything in your body, and it's where your consciousness lives. So, damaging, it is a big deal. But if you get a brain injury, it's remarkably good at compensating for any losses.
9. **We Know What Will Make Us Happy or Sad:** We all probably have a pretty good idea of what we enjoy and what we don't. But, actually, when it comes down to it, we have no control over what scenarios and experiences make us happy or sad in the moment.
10. **Listening to Mozart Makes You Smart:** The study widely considered as controversial. Researchers say the students didn't get any smarter, but they just got better at certain tasks. Also, no other scientists have been able to replicate the results.

These things above show the following things:

1. Brain (consciousness) studies are on the way.
2. Most of the mechanisms of brain are under research levels.
3. New understandings of brain mechanisms will be day by day findings.

There is one of idea of consciousness today.

The term "consciousness" is used in two situations; one is when a person is in a generalized condition of awareness with behaviors of knowing and understanding a thing outside of the atmosphere that is directly related with his attention; outer looking. In inner looking, it happens when we think about a thing Inside of ourselves, namely, in one's inside itself. For explaining about these behaviors, there are P-consciousness and A-consciousness. P-consciousness, Eric Lormand states that there are conscious states (Lormand et al, 1999).

1. Conscious perceptual representations.
2. Conscious bodily sensations.
3. Conscious imagining.
4. Conscious streams of thoughts.

A-consciousness is explained by David J. Chalmers (1999) in an example as; all nine letters in a squared array are experienced, but only three can be reported at a time. In this case, only three letter-representations are accessed. So as stated above, A-consciousness is an availability for use in reasoning and rationally guiding speech and action. These two are closely related with each other. Because it can be restated that P-consciousness is mechanisms of presentation of awareness and A-consciousness is mechanisms of choice of attention.

So, the consciousness flow by David J. Chalmers can be restated as follows:

A-consciousness → WHOLE CONSCIOUSNESS → P-consciousness → CONSCIOUSNESS STATE

- **WHOLE CONSCIOUSNESS:** the consciousness entity in brain
- **CONSCIOUSNESS STATE:** the output state from whole consciousness at a certain moment

There is another idea of consciousness.

From the present typical understandings of consciousness in the papers (Angyal, 1941; Lormand, 1999; Sugiyama, 2000), it may be stated that consciousness can be concluded as follows:

1. From the beginning of birth, a primitive organism of consciousness is existed.
2. A consciousness grows by having stimuli internally and externally from brain.
3. A consciousness consists of two:
   a. A consciousness relates with stimuli from outside.
   b. A consciousness which relates with only inside matters of brain.

The above terms of 2 and 3 can be restated as external consciousness and internal consciousness.

External Consciousness behavior:

1. Differentiate an object from input.
2. Recognize an object in a category.
3. Recognize an object what it is.
4. If the recognition meets requirement satisfied, then it is the state of being consciousness.

   Internal Consciousness behavior:

1. Differentiate an object from External consciousness.
2. Recognize the object in a category.
3. Recognize the object what it is.
4. If the output is not satisfied by the expectation, then reflects the object into Internal Consciousness again within a different category.
5. If the reflection meets the requirement satisfied, then it is the state of being consciousness.

MAIN FOCUS OF THE CHAPTER

Issues and Problems

From the previous chapter, the following things can be said:

1. Consciousness is definitely existed inside of brain. Because the level of consciousness is small when human is born. And it may grow when year by year passes.
2. Consciousness comes up to the consciousness state in mind by going through some steps (consciousness states).
3. Consciousness is discontinuous. It does not come up to the consciousness state continuously from one state to the final state (another state).
4. Reflection is something related with consciousness state.
5. A consciousness state is explained but not its mechanism.
6. Complexity of simple functional connections is not the answer for consciousness state in any sense.

   So, it can be said at present that there is not yet a complete understanding of consciousness.

SOLUTIONS AND RECOMMENDATIONS

Even though consciousness mechanisms are vague at present thoughts, the following facts will be the key issues of understanding of consciousness as an entity.

In the paper ("Science Alert", 2018), it says as follows:

Quote:

Undoubtedly the Penrose-Hameroff Orch OR model may be considered as a good theory for describing information processing mechanisms and holistic phenomena in the human brain. The theory explains both physical and biological aspects of consciousness such as

1. *Non-computability of consciousness;*
2. *Relation of consciousness to space-time geometry;*
3. *The role of microtubules as suitable candidates for information processing;*
4. *Mechanisms for macroscopic quantum computing- dendritic webs.*

Microtubules

During the 1970s, Dr. Stewart Hameroff from the University of Arizona, and Dr. Kunio Yasue and Dr. Mari Jibu from the Okayama University started studying the pathways for conscious activity between neural cells. They examined how anesthesia agents such as chloroform and nitrous oxide could disable the consciousness of a patient. In addition, they independently found that consciousness is something to do with a matrix of twisted spiral filaments which they called it tubulins.

So, it is obvious to say that microtubules will be one of solutions for making consciousness state under the thought of artificial entity. Also, the key issue of artificial entity is concurrent processing of data from the five senses and the others of brain.

FUTURE RESEARCH DIRECTIONS

There are many understandings about a consciousness state as typical ones are mentioned in the above sections. However, there are not any that will explain about a consciousness entity itself and its mechanisms. There still needs more understandings about a consciousness entity itself. Of course, it would be said that Microtubules phenomena will be the key to understand a consciousness state and the entity itself.

CONCLUSION

This chapter explains the differences between the present AI and human brain in their functions and their behaviors. The meanings of these differences are discussed and considered. And then the present general understanding of "Consciousness" is argued and described by using Wikipedia and two understanding papers. Also, it tries to find out and to understand the present research direction and its reason about what a consciousness (brain) is. Moreover, as the present understandings about a consciousness state and its entity, it has been concluded that a consciousness, as a whole, is still under important research issue.

REFERENCES

Angyal, A. (1941). *Foundation for a Science of Personality*. Harvard Press.

Chalmers, D. J. (1999). In *The MIT Encyclopedia of the Cognitive Studies*. MIT.

Lormand, E. (1999). In *The MIT Encyclopedia of the Cognitive Studies*. MIT.

Science Alert. (n.d.). There's no such thing as being right or left brained and 9 other brain myths we've all heard. Retrieved from https://www.sciencealert.com/there-s-no-such-thing-as-being-right-or-left-brained-and-9-other-brain-myths-we-ve-all-heard/

Sugiyama, S. (2000). Reflected Method for Having Consciousness. *Paper presented at the IEEE International Conference on Systems, Mand and Cybernetics*. 10.1109/ICSMC.2000.886477

Sugiyama, S. (2001). *Virtual-Space Factory: General Concept Of Holonic Control*. Unpublished doctoral dissertation, University of Gifu, Gifu, Japan.

KEY TERMS AND DEFINITIONS

A-consciousness: Mechanisms of choice of attention.

Attention: One of the brain behaviors that will happen in the second stage for understanding.

Consciousness: One of the brain behaviors for understanding all brain's activities.

Intention: One of the brain behaviors that will happen in the first staged for understanding.

P-consciousness: mechanisms of presentation of awareness.

Perception: One of the brain behaviors that will happen in the third stage for understanding.

Recognition: One of the brain behaviors that will happen in the final stage for understanding.

Chapter 3
General Activities of Brain as Functions

ABSTRACT

Most living creatures have an accumulated neuron processing unit area (ANPUA) in their bodies. Most of them are placed and centered in a head for processing various kinds of information. They behave like a central processing unit (CPU) in a digital computer system from a functional point of view. In this chapter, is described the general activities of the brain as a point of functional behavior. Also covered are the discussion about a digital computer from the same functional point of view.

BACKGROUND

Computer

From 17th century to early 20th century, it is said that those ages are the age of mechanical calculating machines. Gearwheels are simply used for the calculation mechanisms.

In 1930, relay is firstly used for a calculation machine, which is the start of an electric calculation machine. Paper tape is used for programming codes. At this stage, codes like "If, then go to" are not able to be used yet. In 1941, the ABC machine is developed by using a vacuum tube. Binary (0 or 1) is used for a basic calculation method. In 1950, Binary Automatic Computer (BINAC) is developed by EMCC. From this age, a business machine is

DOI: 10.4018/978-1-5225-8217-5.ch003

come up International Business Machines Corporation (IBM) to the world. IBM comes up to the world as a main frame computer company in the first place. After this age, the computers had been becoming small and small in their sizes. In the first the place, a room where a computer was situated at was very large. Since then, the computer rooms had been small and small as computer sizes also had become small and small as described the following:

a huge room → a room → desk size (work station) → desk top → laptop → handy type

→ palm size → wrist size → directly into brain

As computer companies, they are as follows: IBM, CRAY, DEC, Intel, Sun Microsystems, Microsoft, Apple, etc., goes on
As a computer processing speed, it has been going faster and faster:

Kilo Hz → Mega Hz → Giga Hz → Tera Hz → ..... .

As a CPU processing bit, as it follows:

4 bits → 8 bits → 16 bits → 32 bits → 64 bits → ..... .

As a basic functional part of computer, there are the following things: CPU basically consists of Arithmetic Logic Unit (ALU), instruction register (instruction decoder), and index register (data).
In addition to those, there are following things: out storage, peripheral I/O devices, network devices, etc.
Generally speaking, a computer (a digital computer: binary computer) processes a code one by one at CPU. Even though it will be possible to use multi processors as a unit of a system, it cannot be escaped by the fact that each processor of CPU has to manipulate each code one by one. So, a processor speed of CPU is one of the important functions for a digital computer.

Brain

Almost all living creatures in this world have a structural appearance of head, body, legs, and arms. But the figures of those are quite different from one another. They are moving around for living (eating, propagating, moving, and resting).

Most of the living creatures have ANPUA in their bodies. Most of them are placed and centered at brain in a head for processing various kinds of human related information. They behave like a CPU in a digital computer system from a point of functional view. This chapter presents general activities of brain as a point of functional behavior. Briefly speaking, the human brain consists of cerebellum and cerebrum. Cerebrum consists of frontal lobe, parietal lobe, occipital lobe, temporal lobe, and five senses (and extra senses).

By using sets and mapping, the case of human brain can be expressed as follows:

1. EB specifies the finite sets of entity of brain.
2. EP specifies the finite sets of entity of part of brain.
3. IC specifies the finite sets of information of neuron signals from the cerebellum.
4. FL specifies the finite sets of the frontal lobe.
5. PL specifies the finite sets of the parietal lobe.
6. OL specifies the finite sets of the occipital lobe.
7. TL specifies the finite sets of the temporal lobe.
8. FS specifies the finite sets of five senses.
9. SB specifies the finite sets of system of brain.

Brain as Function

The human brain can be expressed by using a function (sets and mapping).

Each set of the parts may behave dependently as well as independently. In another words, a brain has a mechanism as a function which is able to play various matters concurrently. This nature of concurrency makes it possible to process many functions, which will make human behave more matters at the same moment of time. This mechanism will also be connected to and to relate with a consciousness state and a consciousness behavior, which will appear and happen at a prefrontal lobe.

Therefore, generally speaking, the following expressions will be given for a human brain as a functional point of view.

SB = (EB, EP)

EB = (EB: IC, FL, PL, OL, TL → EB(IC, FL, PL, OL, TL))

EP = (EP: IC, FL, PL, OL, TL → EP(IC, FL, PL, OL, TL))

where → denotes mapping.

MAIN FOCUS OF THE CHAPTER

Differences between Wet Bain and Dry Brain

There are typical functional differences between wet brain and dry brain. Those are described as follows;

1. A computer (a digital computer) processes a code (program) one by one at CPU. On the other hand, a brain processes various matters concurrently. Each part of brain can be processed dependently as well as independently.
2. A computer system can do many things like calculation, control, management, various kinds of processing assistance (word processor, illustration, CAD & CAM, etc.), medical assistance, and human assistance. And a computer can do them very fast. On the other hand, a brain can do the same things but slower than a computer.
3. A computer system is not able to have a mind and a consciousness. On the other hand, a brain has them. Therefore, it is possible to play an advanced matter like think out, deduction, state comprehension, state inference, etc.
4. A computer system is able to connect with huge numbers of systems, but a brain is able to connect with a limited number of matters.

CONCLUSION

The chapter Investigates general activities of brain as a point of functional behavior and argued about a digital computer as it is. It argues about the differences between a brain (wet Brain) and a digital computer (dry brain) whether there is any or not. If there is any difference, the difference will be deepened for further study in order to find out the major functions that make the difference. Those are typical functional differences between wet brain and dry brain is compared.

KEY TERMS AND DEFINITIONS

ALU: Arithmetic Logic Unit. The heart of CPU that treats arithmetic function.

CPU: Central Processing Unit. The main mechanism and the function for a digital computer.

Instruction Register: Instruction decoder in the CPU for treating instruction sets.

Chapter 4

Wet Consciousness and Dry Consciousness

ABSTRACT

In this chapter, wet consciousness and dry consciousness will be defined. For doing the definitions, it illustrates the differences between wet consciousness and dry consciousness under the understandings at present. Wet consciousness is a living creature brain and dry consciousness is an entity made by a digital computer. Naturally, consciousness itself is also argued on what it is and on its general understanding of mechanisms. And then, it presents about the wet Consciousness mechanisms. In addition, the possibility to create dry consciousness will be studied under these situations.

INTRODUCTION

Consciousness is a current and vivid issue (study) at present. It has been a long history behind, but it is not yet come up to a clear explanation on it.

A human in the living creatures is picked up for the wet consciousness study here. As a dry consciousness, a usual computer system is argued first and then discuss the computer system which has a similar function as wet consciousness.

DOI: 10.4018/978-1-5225-8217-5.ch004

BACKGROUND

Humans have one of the most complex creature systems in this world. The human is a brain centered creature in a sense that every movement of human related thoughts is done through by the brain. Namely, almost every part of human body is controlled and managed by brain. In this sense, human is a brain centered creature. In these processes of the behaviors, human does necessary things for himself, like eating, looking, walking, talking, etc. (living and working activities). In these living and working activities, a consciousness phenomenon (wet consciousness) is come up to in mind.

A computer system is also able to do same kind of activities like human. But it does not seem that a computer system does these activities with a consciousness phenomenon (dry consciousness).

MAIN FOCUS OF THE CHAPTER

Wet Consciousness and Dry Consciousness

Firstly, here defines wet consciousness and dry consciousness consulting by Wikipedia ("Consciousness," n.d.)

Definitions of consciousness; wet consciousness and dry Consciousness.

Wet Consciousness

Almost every living creature (mammals) has a kind of a consciousness state. It is the state of awareness, of being aware of an external object or something within itself. It is the ability to experience or to feel, wakefulness, and having a sense of selfhood or soul.

Dry Consciousness

It is called artificial consciousness, machine consciousness, or synthetic consciousness. Especially this concept is used in robotics and AI research areas.

It is the state of awareness, of being aware of an external object or something within itself. It is the ability to experience or to feel, wakefulness, and having a sense of selfhood or soul.

Wet consciousness is possible to exist as it is with human. However, dry consciousness is not yet possible to have the following states; awareness, experience, feel, wakefulness, selfhood, soul.

CONSCIOUSNESS IN GENERAL

Consciousness itself is a current and vivid issue at present even now. It has been a long history behind, but it is not yet come up to a clear explanation on it.

As a primitive and basic human brain structure, the following tissues (parts of brain) can be considered:

1. Cerebellum as the very primitive desires and the life maintenance movements
2. Cerebrum as the advanced neuron processes including the prefrontal cortex by receiving the neuron information through cerebellum
3. Prefrontal cortex
4. Five senses

Also, it is known that a consciousness comes up in a prefrontal cortex of a cerebrum. As a functional flow, any desire from the cerebellum goes to the cerebrum. Namely, the cerebrum as the advanced neuron processes including the prefrontal cortex and the five senses will be receiving the neuron information through the cerebellum. In this neuron flow, there comes up a consciousness state at the prefrontal cortex.

The above explanation will be rewritten functionally.

Information from cerebellum

→ cerebrum (frontal lobe + parietal lobe + occipital lobe + temporal lobe)
→ action

This may be transformed into a functional expression by using sets theory, which may be possible to re-express as dry consciousness.

CONCLUSION

Wet consciousness and dry consciousness are defined in order to argue about the differences between wet consciousness and dry consciousness under the understandings at present. In addition, it is argued about the wet consciousness mechanisms. And then, the possibility to create dry consciousness at present is studied.

REFERENCES

Wikipedia. (n.d.). Consciousness. Retrieved from https//en.wikipedia.org/wiki/Consciousness

KEY TERMS AND DEFINITIONS

Dry Consciousness: It is called artificial consciousness, machine consciousness, or synthetic consciousness. This concept is used in robotics and AI research areas. It is the state of awareness, of being aware of an external object or something within itself. It is the ability to experience or to feel, wakefulness, and having a sense of selfhood or soul.

Wet Consciousness: Almost every living creature (mammals) has a kind of a consciousness state. It is the state of awareness, of being aware of an external object or something within itself. It is the ability to experience or to feel, wakefulness, and having a sense of selfhood or soul.

Chapter 5
Case of a Person on Consciousness Levels

ABSTRACT

This chapter introduces the consciousness studies through caring for (attending-to) highly aged person (CFHAP). Also, it talks about the novel knowledge obtained through CFHAP on brain activities related to matters of a cerebrum and a cerebellum. Through a highly aged person's attending-to, it happened coincidentally that it was noticed curious brain behaviors in the from-awake-to-sleep process. They might be related with a consciousness state, mind, intention, attention, perception, recognition, understanding, and action. From these behaviors, it might be also possible to understand some of the brain mechanisms in a consciousness state and a mind state. In these regards, this chapter will show patient symptoms, bodily movements, and behaviors.

INTRODUCTION

Through a highly aged person's attending-to, it happened coincidentally to notice the curious brain behaviors in the from-awake-to-sleep process. They might be related with a consciousness state, mind, intention, attention, perception, recognition, understanding, and action. From these behaviors, it might be also possible to understand some of the brain mechanisms in a consciousness state and a mind state.

DOI: 10.4018/978-1-5225-8217-5.ch005

In these regards, this chapter will show a patient symptoms, bodily movements, and behaviors.

It will be noticed that there are many and much differences among a sleep state, a deep sleep state, and a Rapid Eye Movement (REM) state, and an awake state. The differences will be vivid neurons active parts of brain which have been heavily activated and non-active parts of brain which have been silently behaved. And those differences will be explained by using the brain parts like cerebrum, cerebellum, etc. And some brand new facts about these differences will be given by as a notion.

BACKGROUND

The patient's medical and vital data information as following:

1. Age and accident:
   a. Age: around mid-ninety.
   b. Accident: fallen down onto floor and broken left thigh.
   c. Mental state: had an indistinct consciousness.
2. Medical information:
   a. Start having taken meals from the 2nd day after the accident, and the one was assisted and helped only by the family for the meals.
   b. Had operation on the 6th day after the accident on the left thigh.
   c. Successful.
   d. Left hospital 3 months later.
3. Vital Data Information
   a. First day at hospital, blood glucose level was around 700.
   b. Eyesight could only recognize bright or dark.
   c. Had a weak consciousness.
   d. Simple communication method was possible only by the eyelids (open or close).
4. After 2 years from left the hospital
   a. Vital Data of the one is almost all good including blood glucose level 113 (waking up time value).
   b. Has almost a fairly distinct consciousness.
   c. Eyesight is still weak but is able to eat meals by oneself.

Patient symptom for the first year at home:

1. In the bed during sleep, the one always has Rapid Eye Movement (REM).
2. In the REM, the one groans and sometimes screams.
3. If the one is woken up in the REM by calling the one's name, the one instantly wakes up without any trouble.
4. As soon as the one lies down on bed, the one starts being in REM.
5. When the one groans and screams, only the craw answers in the distance? (not for sure).
6. For more than a year, the one had not had deep sleep.

Patient symptom at present at home:

1. The one can have a deep sleep.
2. REM does not come up soon after the one start sleeping.
3. Taking meals by one-self with using one's own hands.
4. Has a distinctive consciousness. However, the one sometimes shows own desires out by using a few words only (: retrieved knowledge of speaking: is able to speak fairly).
5. Has a difficulty of walking by one-self. The one needs much assistance for walking.

MAIN FOCUS OF THE CHAPTER

Relationships Among Cerebrum, Cerebellum, First Person, Second Person, Consciousness, Controversies, and Problems

The reason why the one has the symptoms as mentioned in the previous chapter will be introduced. Those are summarized again below:

1. In the bed during sleep, the one always has Rapid Eye Movement (REM).
2. In the REM, the one groans and sometimes screams.
3. If the one is woken up in the REM by calling the one's name, the one instantly wakes up without any trouble.
4. As soon as the one lies down on bed, the one starts being in REM.

5.   When the one groans and screams, only the craw answers in the distance? (not for sure).
6.   For more than a year, the one had not had deep sleep.

As a primitive and basic human brain structure, the following tissues (parts of brain) are considered:

1.   Cerebellum as the very primitive desires and the life maintenance movements
2.   Cerebrum as the advanced neuron processes including the prefrontal cortex by receiving the neuron information through cerebellum
3.   Prefrontal cortex
4.   Five senses

During the REM state, the one does not seem to have a consciousness state. Due to the one definitely has no sight view from the outside stimuli, no responses with the outside stimuli like by small callings, soft and gentle touching, etc. Only the one does is to groan and screaming (calling). It seems that the neuron information comes from cerebellum directly to for actions. Naturally, some of the body parts are moving, so it seems that the primary motor cortex and the five senses are in active too. In this state, only First Person is in an active state, but it is not with the consciousness state. However, when the one is woken up by big voices or by tapping (shaking) the hands, the one wakes up and can answer by questions. This phenomenon will show that the one will wake up under a consciousness state by occurring "Reflection State in the cerebrum". Namely, the tapping or the big voices (reflection) may deduce some kinds of actions in the cerebrum.

It may be said that the following thing.

[**Notion 5-1:** *Reflection occurs in the cerebrum. This may cause some processing in the cerebrum.*]

From the further deduction, it would be considered that Second Person will come up to only when the neuron information goes to Cerebrum. And at this stage, a consciousness will come up to the consciousness state (with a mind).

From the above arguments, it is natural to come to the following two conclusions about the neuron information flow on the primitive human desires from the cerebellum.

Information (Neuron Signal) Flow Inside Brain

1.   Case 1: Cerebellum → 5 Senses → Action

First person is only in active state without a consciousness state.

2.   Case 2: Cerebellum → Cerebrum (+ 5 senses) → Action

First person and second person are in the active states with a consciousness state.

It would be possible to have the following notions:

*[**Notion 5-2:** Generally speaking, there are two types of the neuron information flows on the primitive human desires from the cerebellum in the brain. The first one is the following.*

1.   Case 1: Cerebellum → 5 Senses → Action

First person is only in the active state without a consciousness state. In another words, all behaviors in this state will not be able to be recognized by the first person in the consciousness state. Namely, all behaviors in this state are under no mind and uncontrolled.]

*[**Notion 5-3:** Generally speaking, there are two types of the neuron information flows on the primitive human desires from the cerebellum in the brain. The second one is the following.*

2.   Case 2: Cerebellum → Cerebrum (+ 5 senses) → Action

First Person and Second Person are in the active states with a consciousness state. In another words, all behaviors in this state will be able to be recognized by the First Person. And the Second Person will be able to be recognized by the First Person. Namely, the First Person will be an Entity and the Second Person will be the Virtual Image (Virtual Entity).]

*[**Notion 5-4:** Second person will be able to be recognized only by first person at a prefrontal cortex in a consciousness state.]*

*[**Notion 5-5:** Mind (a consciousness state) does not come up to only under First person.]*

FUTURE RESEARCH DIRECTIONS

It is very important to examine the following matters experimentally:

1. A neuron flow of cerebellum is only one directionally going to a cerebrum?
2. A consciousness state does not come up to at all when a prefrontal cortex is not working?
3. First person comes up without a consciousness at all?
4. Second person together with first person comes up to only with a consciousness state?

CONCLUSION

Here studied about the consciousness studies through CFHAP. Also, studied about the novel knowledge will be obtained through CFHAP on brain activities related with matters of a cerebrum and a cerebellum.

The following results are given as the notions:

*[**Notion 5-1:** Reflection occurs in the cerebrum. This may cause the processing in the cerebrum.]*

*[**Notion 5-2:** Generally speaking, there are two types of the neuron information flows on the primitive human desires from the cerebellum in the brain. The first one is the following.*

1. **Case 1:** Cerebellum → 5 Senses → Action

First person is only in the active state without a consciousness state. In another words, all behaviors in this state will not be able to be recognized by the first person in the consciousness state. Namely, all behaviors in this state are under no mind and uncontrolled.]

41

[**Notion 5-3:** *There are two types of the neuron information flows on the primitive human desires from the cerebellum in the brain. The second one is the following.*

2.   **Case 2:** Cerebellum → Cerebrum (+ 5 senses) → Action

First person and second person are in the active states with a consciousness state. In another words, all behaviors in this state will be able to be recognized by the first person. In addition, the second person will be able to be recognized by the first person. Namely, the first person will be an entity and the second person will be the virtual image (virtual entity).]

[**Notion 5-4:** *Second person will be able to be recognized only by first person at a prefrontal cortex in a consciousness state.*]

[**Notion 5-5:** *Mind (a consciousness state) does not come up to only under first person.*]

KEY TERMS AND DEFINITIONS

Cerebellum: The very primitive desires and the life maintenance movements will occur.

Cerebrum: It consists of frontal lobe, parietal lobe, occipital lobe, and temporal lobe.

Highly Aged Person: The person who is over 75 years old.

Chapter 6
Human Behavior as First Person

ABSTRACT

This chapter introduces first person known as the grammatical person (first person, second person, third person) basically and then goes over a theoretical argument of first person in a frame work of brain activities (cerebrum, cerebellum) as they are known and understood now. And then, the arguments will go to a practical argument by using the novel knowledge as shown in the chapter 5. In this way, it will be further studied and will be more deepened in order to get the general basic brain functions of first person. They will be described as a notion on first person.

BACKGROUND AND INTRODUCTION

Wikipedia says about the grammatical person of first person as follows ("Grammatical Person," n.d.)

Quote:

Grammatical person, in linguistics, is the grammatical distinction between deictic references to participant(s) in an event; typically, the distinction is among the speaker (first person), the addressee (second person), and others (third person). Put in simple colloquial English, first person is that which includes the speaker, namely, I, we, me, and us., second person is the person

DOI: 10.4018/978-1-5225-8217-5.ch006

or people spoken to, literally, you, and third person is the other people, namely, he, she, they and them.

In this chapter, it will be argued and studied how this grammatical first person comes out in human brain by using some of the understandings out of the patient behaviors from the previous chapter.

MAIN FOCUS OF THE CHAPTER

Issues of First Person, Controversies, and Problems

First person whether there are any brain activities as first person or not is introduced.

In the chapter 5, the following notions are given by:

*[**Notion 5-1:** Reflection occurs in the cerebrum. This may cause a processing in the cerebrum.]*

*[**Notion 5-2:** Generally speaking, there are two types of the neuron information flows on the primitive human desires from the cerebellum in the brain. The first one is the following.*

1. **Case 1:** Cerebellum → 5 Senses → Action

First person is only in the active state without a consciousness state. In another words, all behaviors in this state will not be able to be recognized by the first person in the consciousness state. Namely, all behaviors in this state are under no mind and uncontrolled.]

*[**Notion 5-3:** There are two types of the neuron information flows on the primitive human desires from the cerebellum in the brain. The second one is the following.*

2. **Case 2:** Cerebellum → Cerebrum (+ 5 senses) → Action

First person and second person are in the active states with a consciousness state. In another words, all behaviors in this state will be able to be recognized by the First Person. Also, the second person will be able to be recognized by the first person. Namely, the first person will be an entity and the second person will be the virtual image (virtual entity).]

[**Notion 5-4:** *Second person will be able to be recognized only by first person at a prefrontal cortex in a consciousness state.*]

[**Notion 5-5:** *Mind (a consciousness state) does not come up to with only first person.*]

By rewriting the above notions, they are as follows:

1. Information (neuron signal) flow inside brain.
    a. **Case 1:** Cerebellum → 5 Senses in Frontal Cortex → Action

First person is only in the active state.

    b. **Case 2:** Cerebellum → Cerebrum (Prefrontal Cortex + 5 senses) → Action

First person and second person are in the active states.

In REM state, it may be said that there must be a certain entity (entity or virtual entity) which is able to show the one's desires like "want to go to toilet", "want to eat something", "want to wake up and to sit on the wheel chair", "want to take a shower", etc. by using one's part of the body like tapping a thing by hands or tapping the wall by hands. It can be said clearly that this is a human behavior and that this human behavior will be acted and be controlled as only a harmonized entity. It will not be hard to deduce that this entity is not a virtual entity (or a virtual image) but it is a real entity. It will be just "the one-self" of person.

So, the following definition will be allowed to express as a notion.

6-1 Definition of first person (notion 6-1): First person is one of the human entities existed in a brain. It behaves under the primitive desires which are originated and come from the cerebellum. The primitive desires will go and act with the primary motor cortex and the five senses. This behavior may be usually acted under without a consciousness and a consciousness state.

However, it may also be acted under with a consciousness and a consciousness state.

FUTURE RESEARCH DIRECTIONS

There are some further research issues as follows:

1. First person is defined in the above. Also, it is recognized under the prefrontal cortex with the second person. The first person is exactly the same as the first person that is recognized in the prefrontal cortex?
2. The first person is an entity. Is it possible to grow by itself?
3. The first person is an entity. The entity itself will grow by getting more information from neuron activities?
4. If the first person without the prefrontal cortex is different from the first person within the prefrontal cortex, is there any communication between them?

CONCLUSION

This chapter studied about first person known as the grammatical person (first person, second person, third person) basically. And then the research went to a theoretical argument of first person in a frame work of brain activities (cerebrum, cerebellum) as they are known and understood now. And then, the arguments went to a practical argument by using the novel knowledge as shown in the chapter 5. In this way, it was further studied and was more deepened in order to get the general basic brain functions and behaviors of first person. Also, they were defined as a notion on first person.

REFERENCES

Wikipedia. (n.d.). Grammatical person. Retrieved from https://en.wikipedia.org/wiki/Grammatical_person

KEY TERMS AND DEFINITIONS

Primitive Desire: The desires that are existed in the cerebellum. They are very primitive and basic desires.

Chapter 7
Human Behavior as Second Person

ABSTRACT

This chapter introduces the second person known as the grammatical person (first person, second person, third person) basically and then goes over a theoretical argument of second person in a framework of brain activities (cerebrum, cerebellum) as they are known and understood now. And then, the arguments will go to a practical argument by using the novel knowledge as shown in chapter 5. In this way, it will be further studied and will be more deepened in order to get the general basic brain functions of second person. They will be described as a notion on second person. Some part of the previous chapter will be repeated for the arguments to go smoothly.

BACKGROUND AND INTRODUCTION

Wikipedia says about the grammatical person of second person as follows ("Grammatical Person", n.d.).

Quote:

Grammatical person, in linguistics, is the grammatical distinction between deictic references to participants in an event; typically, the distinction is among the speaker (first person), the addressee (second person), and others (third person). Put in simple colloquial English, first person is that which includes the speaker, namely, I, we, me, and us, second person is the person

DOI: 10.4018/978-1-5225-8217-5.ch007

or people spoken to, literally, you, and the third person is the other person, namely, they, and them.

In this chapter, it will be argued and studied how this grammatical second person comes out in human brain by using some of the understandings out of the patient behaviors.

MAIN FOCUS OF THE CHAPTER

Issues of Second Person, Controversies, Problems

Second person whether there are any brain activities as second person or not is introduced.

In chapter 5 and the chapter 6, the following notions are given:

Notion 5-1: *There are two types of the neuron information flows on the primitive human desires from the cerebellum in the brain. The first one is the following:*

1.   **Case 1:** Cerebellum → 5 Senses → Action

First person is only in the active state without a consciousness state. In another words, all behaviors of the first person in this state will not be able to be recognized by the first person itself in the consciousness state. Namely, all the behaviors of the first person in this state are under no mind and not controlled.

Notion 5-2: *There are two types of the neuron information flows on the primitive human desires from the cerebellum in the brain. The second one is the following.*

2.   **Case 2:** Cerebellum → Cerebrum (+ 5 senses) → Action

First person and second person are in the active states with a consciousness state. In another words, all behaviors of the first person in this state will be able to be recognized by the first person itself. And the second person will be able to be recognized by the first person.

Notion 5-3: *Second person will be able to be recognized only by first person at a prefrontal cortex in a consciousness state.*

Notion 5-4: *Mind does not come up to only under first person.*

Notion 6-1 Definition of first person (definition 6-1): First person is one of the human entities existed in a brain. It behaves under the primitive desires which are originated and come from the cerebellum. The primitive desires will go and act with the primary motor cortex and the five senses. This behavior will be usually acted under without a consciousness and a consciousness state. However, it will also be acted under with a consciousness and a consciousness state.

By rewriting the above notions, they are as follows:

1. Information (neuron signal) flow inside brain.
    a. **Case 1:** Cerebellum → 5 Senses in Frontal Cortex → Action

First person is only in the active state.

    b. **Case 2:** Cerebellum → Cerebrum (Prefrontal Cortex + 5 senses) → Action

First person and second person are in the active states.

In the REM state, it may be said that there must be a certain entity in the one's brain which is able to show the one's desires like want to go to toilet, want to eat and to drink something, want to wake up and to sit on the wheel chair, want to take a shower, etc. by using one's part of the body like tapping a thing by hands or tapping the wall by hands. It can be said clearly that this is a human behavior and that this human behavior will be acted and be controlled as a harmonized only one entity. It will not be hard to deduce that this entity will be just the one-self of the one. Namely, the entity of the one will be first person of the one. This is happening in the Case 1 above.

In the Case 2 above, first person and second person are in the active states. Also, the one is also conscious about another person (the second person). For example, the one is able to say that I want to go to toilet. to the second person by speaking, I want to something to eat. to the second person by speaking, I need to wake up. Get me on the wheel chair. to the second person by speaking, etc. This phenomenon will explain that the first person (the one) is recognizing the second person in the prefrontal cortex. The first person is definitely existed as an entity in the prefrontal cortex. However, the second person is on the prefrontal cortex as to be recognized by the first person. Namely, the second person is not existed as a real entity. Namely, the second person is virtual entity or virtual image in the prefrontal cortex.

As the result of the above arguments, second person will be able to be defined as follows:

7-1 Definition of second person (notion 7-1): The second person is a virtual existence (or a virtual image) which will appear in the prefrontal cortex. Also, the second person is only recognized by the first person in the prefrontal cortex. The first person and the second person will appear in the prefrontal cortex within the consciousness and the consciousness state.

FUTURE RESEARCH DIRECTIONS

Second person may be defined more in detail by explanations of neurons' connections and behaviors. Although, for further studies, there are subjects on the following:

1. Second person seems to appear as a virtual existence (or a virtual image) in the prefrontal cortex of the frontal lobe, which is not an entity like the first person. What sort of connections and relations are existed between them? Because it seems that there should be close relationships between them. The close relationships will appear when the first person and the second person have interacted each other for doing taking-care for a highly aged person, for example.
2. Second person will be memorized as a mass of neurons' connections in the prefrontal cortex?
3. Second person will be a thing or a matter or an object or "a group of neurons"?

CONCLUSION

The chapter presented second person known as the grammatical person basically and then went to a theoretical argument of second person in a frame work of brain activities. And then, the arguments went to a practical argument by using the novel knowledge as shown in the chapter 5 and the chapter 6. In this way, it was further studied and was more deepened in order to get the general basic brain functions of second person. They were described as a definition (a notion) on second person.

REFERENCES

Wikipedia. (n.d.). Grammatical person. Retrieved from https://en.wikipedia.org/wiki/Grammatical_person

Chapter 8
Another Kind as First Person

ABSTRACT

This chapter introduces first person as an artificial entity. Firstly, first person will be defined by using the notions in chapter 6 and chapter 7. Also, the functions of first person will be argued and studied as a point of views of the mechanisms. Secondly, the functions of first person will be transformed into a computer system by using a rough modal method (not The Fourier modal method). This method is simply to replace a function of first person that is discovered as described in chapter 6 and chapter 7 into a modal function of a computer system as an artificial entity. Some part of the previous chapters will be repeated for the arguments to go smoothly.

INTRODUCTION

This chapter is a challenging chapter in a sense that brand new idea comes up for realization of first person. Human naturally has first person in a brain as it is well recognized by oneself autonomously. When in the state of awake or dream, first person comes up to mind in a consciousness state. And it behaves as if the main character of the entity (a human) for the physical body and the mind. As described in the previous chapters 6, 7, and 8, it will be understood that first person appears under the specific conditions. So, this chapter tries to clear up those conditions. And then, those conditions will be transformed into a function, which will be possible to transform into a computer system.

DOI: 10.4018/978-1-5225-8217-5.ch008

BACKGROUND

The reasons why the one has the symptoms as mentioned in the previous chapter are presented as following:

1. In the bed during sleep, the one always (no alternative) has Rapid Eye Movement (REM).

This phenomenon is quite unusual with a reason why a deep sleep does not come up to. Also, REM state is usually brought to a person ten or twenty minutes after sleep or sometime before waking up.

From these facts about REM, this phenomenon will be understood as follows.

   a. The one is simply dreaming all the time.
   b. The brain of the one has been repairing one's own brain all the time during REM sleep by reflecting necessary neuron connections in the prefrontal cortex.
2. In the REM, the one groans and sometimes screams.

he one seems not to understand and not to recognize the outside the world including the second person. So, this phenomenon may be understood that the only first person comes up to the one in this REM state.

3. If the one is woken up in the REM by calling the one's first name, the one instantly wakes up without any trouble and bewilderment.

This shows that the one does not have deep sleep at all. The one is always in REM state when the one is asleep. This is quite unusual.

4. As soon as the one lies down on bed, the one instantly starts being in REM.

This phenomenon may show that the prefrontal cortex is in trouble. This phenomenon also may show that mainly the cerebellum is working. The cerebrum seems not working perfectly well in treating the information from the cerebellum, so that the REM state comes up to do for repairing some ill parts of the prefrontal cortex.

5. When the one groans and screams, only the craws in the distance answer (not for sure) (?).

(This is a kind of laugh. But it seems so!)

6. For more than a year, the one does not have deep sleep (always REM).

This may show that this phenomenon is not the state that had happened only once.

As a primitive and basic human brain structure, the following tissues (parts of brain) are considered in this case:

1. Cerebellum as the very primitive desires and the life maintenance movements,
2. Cerebrum as the advanced neuron processes including the prefrontal cortex by receiving the neuron information through cerebellum,
3. Frontal lobe as the main part in voluntary movement for human behaviors,
4. Prefrontal cortex as the advanced neuron processes for human behaviors,
5. Five senses (there are more Senses but here uses main five senses).

As a neuron signal information flow of the brain in this case, the followings will be generally considered.

1. Information (neuron signal) flow inside brain.
    a. **Case 1:** Cerebellum → Frontal lobe (Primary Motor Cortex + 5 Senses) → Action

It may be said that first person is only able to be in the active state.

    b. **Case 2:** Cerebellum → Cerebrum (Frontal lobe + Parietal lobe + Occipital lobe + Temporal lobe) → Action

It will be said that first person and second person are able to be in the active states.

2. Information (neuron signal) flow from outside world.
    a. No Information from outside world into brain (cerebrum + cerebellum).

During the REM state, the one does not seem to have a consciousness state. Because the one definitely has no sight views from the outside stimuli, no responses with the outside stimuli like calling, touching, etc. Only the one does is to have groans and screaming (calling). It seems that the neuron information comes from Cerebellum directly for the actions.

From the above arguments, it is natural to come to the following conclusion about the neuron information flow from the primitive human desires of the cerebellum in this case.

1. Information (neuron signal) flow inside brain.
   a. **Case 1:** Cerebellum → Primary Motor Cortex + 5 Senses → Action

First person is only able to be in active state. However, it is not sure whether a consciousness state is in active or not. But the primary motor cortex and 5 Senses are only in active, so it will be concluded that a consciousness state is not active.

This situation is very curious in a sense that first person has come up to the one, but it will not be able to be recognized by the one-self.

So, it will be concluded that the information from cerebellum is nothing to do with the consciousness state even though lots of human actions will have come up to by the one.

Now, as a necessary fact about cerebellum mechanisms in this case, it can be easily rewritten by using finites sets as following:

Let,

IC = {information of neuron signals of/from cerebellum}.

And from the arguments above, the first person in the Frontal Lobe will be defined by using finites sets as follows.

FL(first person) = {frontal lobe, first person | IC, primary motor cortex, 5 senses}.

And the above processes will be called Rough Modal Method (RMM).
Here, RMM is defined again by using sets and mapping.

[Rough Modal Method]

General Information (GI) flows are roughly accumulated into a mass flow (Modal Flow (MF)) of information. The masses of flows (Modal Flows) have a loose direction and a general connectivity as a character among them.

By using sets and mapping, the case of brain can be expressed as follows.

1. EB specifies the finite sets of entity of brain.
2. EP specifies the finite sets of entity of part of brain.
3. IC specifies the finite sets of Information of neuron signals of/from cerebellum.
4. PMC specifies the finite sets of primary motor cortex.
5. FS specifies the finite sets of five senses.
6. SB specifies the finite sets of system of brain.

Therefore, the following expressions will be given.

SB = (EB(GI), EP(GI))

EB(GI) = (EB: IC, PMC, FS → EB(MF)(IC, PMC, FS))

EP(GI) = (EP: IC, PMC, FS → EP(MF)(IC, PMC, FS))

where → denotes mapping.

As an example of first person, RMM will be as follows.

SB = (EB(first person), EP(first person))

EB(first person) = (EB: IC, PMC, FS → EB(first person)(IC, PMC, FS))

EP(first person) = (EP: IC, PMC, FS → EP(first person)(IC, PMC, FS))

MAIN FOCUS OF THE CHAPTER

Another Kind in First Person

As argued and discussed in the above section, first person appears in the processes of FL (first person) by RMM. Here talks about the implementation of FL (first person) into a computer system, which is the simplest case of the computer system.

It consists of three units, which are Desires Unit (DU), Process Unit (PU), and Senses Unit (SU).

1.   DU; some kinds of desires continuously flow out to.

This unit has all kinds of human desires as data. They will be simply dispatched and will go out at the certain periods into PU one directionally.

2.   PU; processing mechanisms are always the same. Also, they are happened at the same time.

This unit does a kind of processing between the data from DU and the data from 5 senses

3.   SU; five senses will get data from outside and processes them at the same moment.

This unit does a kind of data gatherings through the five senses.
So, the simplest computer system is as follows.

$$DU \rightarrow PU \leftarrow SU$$

FUTURE RESEARCH DIRECTIONS

As an implementation of the first person, there would be better to have more exact and concrete system explanations. Namely, DU, PU, and SU units will be better to study in the directions of the mechanisms in terms of the connections among the units.

CONCLUSION

First person as an artificial entity is studied. Firstly, first person was defined by using the notions in chapter 6 and chapter 7. Also, the functions of first person were discussed and studied as a point of views of the mechanisms. Secondly, the functions of first person were transformed into a computer system by using a rough modal method (not The Fourier modal method). This method is simply to replace a function of first person that is discovered as described in chapter 6 and chapter 7 into a modal function of a computer system as an artificial entity. And then, there were showed another kind of first person from the knowledge given by the arguments and the study.

KEY TERMS AND DEFINITIONS

DU: Desires Unit. Some kinds of desires continuously flow out to.
PU: Processing Unit. Processing mechanisms.
SU: Senses Unit.

Chapter 9

Another Kind as Second Person

ABSTRACT

This chapter introduces second person as an artificial entity. First, second person will be defined by using the notions in Chapter 6 and chapter 7. Also, the functions of second person will be argued and studied as a point of views of the mechanisms. Second, the functions of second person will be transformed into a computer system by using a rough modal method (not The Fourier modal method). This method is simply to replace a function of second person that is discovered as described in chapter 6 and chapter 7 into a modal function of a computer system as an artificial entity. Some part of the previous chapters will be repeated for the arguments to go smoothly.

INTRODUCTION

This chapter is a challenging chapter in a sense that brand new idea comes up for realization of second person. Human naturally has second person in a brain as it is well recognized by oneself autonomously. When in the state of awake or dream, first person and second person come up to mind in a consciousness state. Also, first person behaves as if the main character of the entity (a human) for the physical body and the mind. Moreover, second person behaves as if an artificial entity (a virtual image) comes up. As described in previous chapters 6, 7, and 8, it will be understood that second person appears under the specific conditions. So, here tries to clear up those

DOI: 10.4018/978-1-5225-8217-5.ch009

conditions. And then, those conditions will be transformed into a function, which will be possible to transform into a computer system.

BACKGROUND

The reason why the one has the symptoms as mentioned in the previous chapter are presented as below:

1. In the bed during sleep, the one always (no alternative) has Rapid Eye Movement (REM).

 This phenomenon is quite unusual in the reason why a deep sleep does not come up to. In addition, REM state is usually brought to a person ten or twenty minutes after sleep or sometime before waking up. From these facts about REM, this phenomenon will be understood as follows.

 a. The one is simply dreaming all the time.
 b. The brain of the one has been repairing one's own brain all the time during REM sleep by reflecting necessary neuron connections in the prefrontal cortex. Under this phenomenon, a consciousness and a consciousness state do not come up to the mind.
2. In the REM, the one groans and sometimes screams.

 The one seems not to understand and not to recognize the outside the world including the second person. So, this phenomenon may be understood that the only first person comes up to the one in this REM state.

3. If the one is woken up in the REM by calling loudly the one's first name, the one instantly wakes up without any trouble and bewilderment.

 This shows that the one does not have deep sleep at all. The one is always in REM state when the one is asleep. This phenomenon is quite unusual.

4. As soon as the one lies down on bed, the one instantly starts being in REM.

This phenomenon may show that the prefrontal cortex is in trouble. This phenomenon also may show that mainly the cerebellum is working. The cerebrum seems not working perfectly well in treating the information from the cerebellum, so that the REM state comes up to do for repairing some ill parts of the prefrontal cortex.

5. When the one groans and screams, only the craws in the distance answer (not for sure) (?).

(This is a kind of laugh. But it seems so!)

6. For more than a year, the one does not have deep sleep (always REM).

This may show that this phenomenon is not the state of only once happened. When the one is awake, the one is under a normal consciousness state.

As a primitive and basic human brain structure, the following tissues (parts of brain) are considered in this case:

1. Cerebellum as the very primitive desires and the life maintenance movements,
2. Cerebrum as the advanced neuron processes including the prefrontal cortex by receiving the neuron information through Cerebellum,
3. Frontal lobe as the main part in voluntary movement for human behaviors,
4. Prefrontal cortex as the advanced neuron processes for human behaviors,
5. Five senses (there are more Senses but here uses main five senses).

As a neuron signal information flow of the brain in this case, the followings will be generally considered.

1. Information (neuron signal) flow inside brain.
    a. Case 1: Cerebellum → Frontal lobe (Primary Motor Cortex + 5 Senses) → Action

It may be said that first person is only able to be in active state.

    b. Case 2: Cerebellum → Cerebrum (Frontal lobe + Parietal lobe + Occipital lobe + Temporal lobe) → Action

It will be said that first person and second person are able to be in the active states.

2. Information (neuron signal) flow from outside world.
    a. No Information from outside world into brain (cerebrum + cerebellum).

During the REM state, the one does not seem to have a consciousness state in awake. Because the one definitely has no sight views from the outside stimuli, no responses with the outside stimuli like small calling, gentle touching, etc. Only the one does is to groans and screaming (calling). It seems that the neuron information comes from cerebellum directly to actions.

On the contrary, the one has a decisive consciousness state when the one is awake. Namely, first person and second person have come up to the mind in a consciousness state with a consciousness. And the one can behave quite natural manners.

From the above arguments, it is natural to come to the following conclusion about the neuron information flows from the primitive human desires of the cerebellum and from the advanced neuron processes of the cerebrum in this case.

So, case 2 will be the information flow inside brain for the one.

1. Information (neuron signal) flow inside brain.
    a. Case 2: Cerebellum → Cerebrum (Frontal lobe + Parietal lobe + Occipital lobe + Temporal lobe) → Action

Now, as a necessary fact about cerebellum and cerebrum mechanisms in this case, it can be easily rewritten by using finites sets as follows.

Let,

IC = {Information of neuron signals of/from cerebellum + cerebrum}.

And from the arguments above, the first person in the Frontal Lobe will be defined by using finites sets as follows.

FL(first person, second person) = {frontal lobe, first person, second person

l IC, frontal lobe, parietal lobe, occipital lobe, temporal lobe, 5 Senses}.

Here, it is rewritten by using RMM by using sets and mapping.

[Rough Modal Method]

General Information (GI) flows are roughly accumulated into a mass flow (Modal Flow (**MF**)) of information. The masses of flows (modal flows) have a loose direction and a general connectivity as a character among them.

By using sets and mapping, the case of brain can be expressed as follows.

1.　**EB** specifies the finite sets of entity of brain.
2.　**EP** specifies the finite sets of entity of part of brain.
3.　**IC** specifies the finite sets of information of neuron signals of/from cerebellum.
4.　**FL** specifies the finite sets of frontal lobe.
5.　**PL** specifies the finite sets of parietal lobe.
6.　**OL** specifies the finite sets of occipital lobe.
7.　**TL** specifies the finite sets of temporal lobe.
8.　**FS** specifies the finite sets of five senses.
9.　**SB** specifies the finite sets of system of brain.

Therefore, the following expressions will be given.

SB = (EB(GI), EP(GI))

EB(GI) = (EB: IC, FL, PL, OL, TL → EB(MF)(IC, FL, PL, OL, TL))

EP(GI) = (EP: IC, FL, PL, OL, TL → EP(MF)(IC, FL, PL, OL, TL))

Where → denotes mapping.

As an example of first person and second person, RMM will be as follows.

SB = (EB(first person), **EP**(first person))

EB(first person, second person) = (**EB: IC, FL, PL, OL, TL**

→ **EB**(first person, second person)(IC, FL, PL, OL, TL))

EP(first person, second person) = (**EP: IC, FL, PL, OL, TL**

→ **EP**(first person, second person)(IC, FL, PL, OL, TL))

MAIN FOCUS OF THE CHAPTER

Issues, Controversies, Problems

As argued and discussed in the above section, second person appears in the processes of FL (second person) by RMM. Here talks about the implementation of FL (second person) into a computer system, which is the most simple case of the computer system.

It consists of four units, which are Desires Unit (DU), Process Unit (PU), Senses Unit (SU), and Prefrontal Cortex Unit (PCU).

1.　DU; some kinds of desires continuously flow out to.

This unit has all kinds of human desires as data. They will be simply dispatched and will go out at the certain periods into PU one directionally.

2.　PU; processing mechanisms are always the same. Also, they are happened at the same time.

This unit does a kind of processing between the data from DU and the data from 5 senses

3.　SU; five senses will get data from outside and processes them at the same moment.

This unit does a kind of data gatherings through the five senses.

4.　PCU; the advanced data processes unit of the prefrontal cortex for human behaviors. This unit manages and deals with an abstract data like consciousness, mind, emotion, feeling, linguistics, and many other human behaviors related data.

Second person will appear in the following state. In this state, first person will also appear and a consciousness state will also come up to.

DU → PCU → PU ← SU.

FUTURE RESEARCH DIRECTIONS

As an implementation of the second person, there would be better to have more exact and concrete system explanations. Namely, four DU, PU, SU, PCU units will be better to study in the directions of the mechanisms in terms of the connections among the units.

CONCLUSION

Second person as an artificial entity is studied. Firstly, second person was defined by using the notions in the chapter 6, the chapter 7, and the chapter 8. Also, the functions of second person were argued and studied as a point of views of the mechanisms. Secondly, the functions of second person were transformed into a computer system by using a rough modal method (not The Fourier modal method). This method is simply to replace a function of second person that is discovered as described in chapter 6, chapter 7, and chapter 8 into a modal function of a computer system as an artificial entity.

And then, there showed another kind of second person from the knowledge given by the arguments and the study above.

Chapter 10
Another Kind in Consciousness

ABSTRACT

This chapter introduces an artificial entity, which may have a consciousness state. The ideas of first person and second person in this book chapter will be cored and used basically for an implementation of the entity. First, a general description of the entity will be argued and discussed again by using the notions in Chapter 6 and Chapter 7. And then the general structure of the entity will be roughly shown by using RMM and the notions from Chapter 6, Chapter 7, Chapter 8, and Chapter 9. Second, the simplest example by using the entity will be given by RMM. Finally, it will be evaluated. Some part of the previous chapters will be repeated for the arguments to go smoothly.

INTRODUCTION

This chapter is the most challenging chapter in a sense that brand new idea comes up for realization of the entity that has a consciousness state. When in the state of awake or dream, a consciousness state comes up to mind as a natural phenomenon. And it behaves as if it were the main character of the entity (a human) for the physical body and the mind. As described in the previous chapters 6, 7, and 8, it will be understood that a consciousness state appears under the usual wakening conditions. So, here tries to clear up those conditions. And then, those conditions will be transformed into a function, which will be possible to transform into a computer system.

DOI: 10.4018/978-1-5225-8217-5.ch010

BACKGROUND

This chapter shows about the phenomenon and the reasons why the one has the symptoms as mentioned in the previous chapters. Those are reconsidered and rewritten again below:

1. In the bed during sleep, the one always (no alternative) has Rapid Eye Movement (REM).

    This phenomenon is quite unusual in a reason why a deep sleep does not come up to. REM state is usually brought to a person ten or twenty minutes after sleep or sometime before waking up. From these facts about REM, this phenomenon will be understood as follows.

    a. The one is simply dreaming all the time.
    b. The brain of the one has been repairing one's own brain all the time during REM sleep by reflecting necessary neuron connections in the prefrontal cortex.
    c. There would be another understanding. The weak consciousness state comes up for a while. And then it disappears for a while in a moment sleep. The repetitions of these states have been occurring.
    d. This is a merging state of consciousness and unconsciousness.
    e. Both cerebrum and cerebellum are active in a weak state.
2. In the REM, the one groans and sometimes screams.

    The one seems not to understand and not to recognize the outside the world including the second person (the one's son) just beside the bed. So, this phenomenon will show that the only first person comes up to the one in this REM state under the groans and the screams. It would be also understood that cerebellum is only in an active state with the primary motor cortex and the five senses.

    From the above arguments, it will be understood that first person comes up to under the cerebellum, the primary motor cortex, and the five senses. Under these states, a consciousness is not an active state.

3. If the one is woken up in the REM by calling the one's first name, the one instantly wakes up without any trouble and bewilderment.

This shows that the one does not have deep sleep at all. The one is always in REM state when the one is asleep. This is quite unusual phenomenon. So, from these facts, it would be understood that this is the merging state of consciousness and unconsciousness. And so, cerebellum is always in an active state and cerebrum is an active state in moment and weakly.

4.   As soon as the one lies down on bed, the one instantly starts being in REM.

This phenomenon may show that the prefrontal cortex is in trouble. This phenomenon also may show that mainly the cerebellum is working in this state. The cerebrum seems not working perfectly well in treating the information from the cerebellum, so that the REM state comes up to do for repairing some ill parts of the prefrontal cortex. This phenomenon will show that a consciousness state and unconsciousness state are merged someway.

5.   When the one groans and screams, only the craws in the distance answer (not for sure) (?).

(This is a kind of laugh. But it seems so!)

6.   For more than a year, the one does not have deep sleep (always REM).

This may show that this phenomenon is not the state of only once happened. When the one is awake, the one is under a normal consciousness state.

As a primitive and basic human brain structure, the following tissues (parts of brain) are considered in this case:

1.   Cerebellum as the very primitive desires and the life maintenance movements,
2.   Cerebrum as the advanced neuron processes including the prefrontal cortex by receiving the neuron information through Cerebellum,
3.   Frontal lobe as the main part in voluntary movement for human behaviors,
4.   Prefrontal cortex as the advanced neuron processes for human behaviors,
5.   Five senses (there are more senses in human body but here uses mainly. The five senses (five Senses)).

As a neuron signal information flow of the brain in this case, the followings will be generally considered.

1. Information (neuron signal) flow inside brain.
    a. **Case 1:** Cerebellum → Frontal lobe (Primary Motor Cortex + 5 Senses) → Action

It may be said that first person is only able to be in an active state. In this state, there will not appear a consciousness state.

    b. **Case 2:** Cerebellum → Cerebrum (Frontal lobe + Parietal lobe + Occipital lobe + Temporal lobe) → Action

It will be said that first person and second person are able to be in the active states. Also, a consciousness state always appears. It will be concluded that second person only will appear when a consciousness state comes up to. In addition, only when second person is recognized, first person is also recognized in a consciousness state.

2. Information (neuron signal) flow from the outside world.
    a. No Information from the outside world into brain (cerebrum + cerebellum) in this case.

During the REM state, the one does not seem to have a consciousness state in awake. Because the one definitely has no sight views from the outside stimuli, no responses with the outside stimuli like small calling, gentle touching, etc. Only the one does is to groan and screaming (calling). It seems that the neuron information comes from cerebellum directly to actions. And it will be understood that this is the very primitive state of first person.

On the contrary, the one has a decisive consciousness state when the one is awake. Namely, first person and second person have come up to the mind in this state. And the one can behave quite in natural manners.

From the above arguments, it is natural to come to the following conclusion about the neuron information flows from the primitive human desires of the cerebellum and from the advanced neuron processes of the cerebrum in this case.

The case 2 will be the information flow inside brain for the one when the one is awake with a consciousness state. Also, it is shown below.

1.   Information (neuron signal) flow inside brain.
     a.   **Case 2:** Cerebellum → Cerebrum (Frontal lobe + Parietal lobe + Occipital lobe + Temporal lobe) → Action

Now, as a necessary fact about cerebellum and cerebrum mechanisms in this case, it can be easily rewritten by using finites sets as follows.
Let,

ICC = {information of neuron signals of/from cerebellum + cerebrum}.

In addition, from the arguments above, the first person and the second person in the Frontal Lobe (FL) will be defined by using finites sets as follows.

FL (first person, second person) = {frontal lobe, first person, second person

I ICC, frontal lobe, parietal lobe, occipital lobe, temporal lobe, 5 Senses}.

It is rewritten by using RMM by using sets and mapping.

[Rough Modal Method]

General Information (**GI**) flows are roughly accumulated into a mass flow (Modal Flow (**MF**)) of information. The masses of flows (modal flows) have a loose direction and a general connectivity as a character among them.
By using sets and mapping, the case of brain can be expressed as follows.

1.   **EB** specifies the finite sets of entity of brain.
2.   **EP** specifies the finite sets of entity of part of brain.
3.   **IC** specifies the finite sets of information of neuron signals of/from cerebellum.
4.   **FL** specifies the finite sets of frontal lobe.
5.   **PL** specifies the finite sets of parietal lobe.
6.   **OL** specifies the finite sets of occipital lobe.
7.   **TL** specifies the finite sets of temporal lobe.
8.   **FS** specifies the finite sets of five senses.
9.   **SB** specifies the finite sets of system of brain.

Therefore, the following expressions will be given.

SB = (EB(GI), EP(GI))

EB(GI) = (EB: IC, FL, PL, OL, TL → EB(MF)(IC, FL, PL, OL, TL))

EP(GI) = (EP: IC, FL, PL, OL, TL → EP(MF)(IC, FL, PL, OL, TL))

Where → denotes mapping.
As an example of first person and second person, RMM will be as follows.

SB = (EB(first person), **EP**(first person))

EB(first person, second person) = (**EB: IC, FL, PL, OL, TL**

→ **EB**(first person, second person)(IC, FL, PL, OL, TL))

EP(first person, second person) = (**EP: IC, FL, PL, OL, TL**

→ **EP**(first person, second person)(IC, FL, PL, OL, TL))

In the case of a consciousness state, it is understood that a consciousness state comes up to only when the second person appears. So, the above RMM equations of **EB** and **EP** will show a System of Brain (**SB**) in a consciousness state under the condition of series of moment **MF**.

MAIN FOCUS OF THE CHAPTER

Another Kind in Consciousness

As argued and discussed in the above section, first Person and second Person will appear in the processes of FL (first person, Second Person) under the condition of series of moment **MF**. Here talks about the implementation of FL (first person, second person) into a computer system, which is the most simple case of a computer system.

It consists of four units, which are Desires Unit (DU), Primitively Structured World Unit (PSWU), Senses Unit (SU), and Prefrontal Cortex Unit (PCU).

1.   DU; some kinds of desires continuously flow out to.

This unit has all kinds of human desires as data. They will be simply dispatched and will go out at the certain periods into PCU one directionally.

2.   PSWU; data from DU, SU, and PCU are processed through this processing mechanism. This processing mechanism has a primitively structured world, which is roughly imitated and projected imagery space through the five senses in real time. This roughly imitated and projected imagery space has been structured flashed moment by moment with data from DU, SU, and PCU. And they happen to be processed at the same series of moment of time. So, this unit does a kind of processing among the data from DU, the data from PCU, and the data from the five senses.

3.   SU; the five senses will get data from outside and processes them at the same moment.

This unit does a kind of data gatherings through the five senses.

4.   PCU; the advanced data processes unit of the prefrontal cortex for human behaviors. This unit manages and deals with an abstract data like consciousness, mind, emotion, feeling, linguistics, and many other human behaviors related data.

As the result of this, the information flow from the cerebellum in the case of first person and second person with a consciousness state will be taking the following states.

1.   First person

First person will appear in the following state. In this state, a consciousness does not appear.

DU → PSWC ← SU.

2.   Second person

Second person will appear in the following state. In this state, first person will also appear and a consciousness state will also come up to.

DU → PCU → PSWC ← SU.

FUTURE RESEARCH DIRECTIONS

As an implementation of the second person, there would be better to have more exact and concrete system explanations. That is to say, four DU, PSWC, SU, PCU units will be better to study in the directions of the mechanisms in terms of the connections among the units.

CONCLUSION

The chapter studied an artificial entity which may have a consciousness state. The ideas of first person and second person in this book chapter was cored and used basically for an implementation of the entity. Firstly, a general description of the entity was argued and discussed again by using the notions and the study results in chapter 6, chapter 7, chapter 8, and chapter 9. And then the general structure of the entity was roughly shown by using RMM and the notions and the study results from chapters 6, chapter 7, chapter 8, and chapter 9. And then, secondly the simplest example by using the entity was given by RMM. And the finally, it was evaluated.

KEY TERMS AND DEFINITIONS

Artificial Entity: Man made thing that has real existence.

DU: Desires unit. Some kinds of desires continuously flow out to.

First Person: First person is one of the human entities existing in a brain. It behaves under the primitive desires which are originated and come from the cerebellum. The primitive desires will go and act with the primary motor cortex and the five senses. This behavior may be usually acted under without a consciousness and a consciousness state. However, it may also be acted under with a consciousness and a consciousness state.

PCU: Prefrontal cortex unit. The advanced data processes unit of the prefrontal cortex for human behaviors.

PSWU: Primitively structured world unit. Data from DU, SU, and PCU are processed through this processing mechanism.

REM: Rapid eye movement.

Second Person: The second person is a virtual existence that will appear in the prefrontal cortex. Also, the second person is only recognized by the first person in the prefrontal cortex. The first person and the second person will appear in the prefrontal cortex within the consciousness and the consciousness state.

SU: Senses unit. The five senses.

Chapter 11
Future Works

ABSTRACT

The chapters will be concluded in the directions of the future works in general. In addition, some of the important factors for the further studies will be extracted and argued on the views of mechanisms and connections. Also, some of the important augmented groups of neurons will be picked up and then introduced with future studies, especially on brand new functions and mechanisms. Moreover, as related matters, some of the concepts (for example, good, bad, like, dislike, love, affection, reflection, etc.) will be introduced for further study. Finally, the human brain will be wrapped up for further study.

FUTURE WORKS

Firstly, all over the chapters are wrapped up.

From the past of 17th century or from the Greek time, the idea of an autonomous machine was started to be brought about a new thought out. Since then, this idea has been evolutionary grown up through pure research; Control → Automatic Control → Intelligent System → Knowledge Base → Dynamic Knowledge Base → Initial AI → Cloud → AI (in General) → Human Like AI → Consciousness (under Studies).

And then, the current researches are going further to study consciousness for the goal of the implementation to a mimicked system of human. These flows of the histories are described in the chapters 1 through 10. Also, in the final chapter 11, the most important further studies' matters, subjects, and words are considered briefly.

DOI: 10.4018/978-1-5225-8217-5.ch011

It shows the most important further studies' matters, subjects, and words:

1.   First person in the mechanisms and the connections.

This comes up as a real entity in the brain. Also, it, itself, will be able to grow by the stimulations from the outside world. So, it is very important to know the mechanisms of the growing and the whole connections for the growing.

2.   Second person in the mechanisms and the connections.

This comes up in the prefrontal cortex as an artificial entity (a virtual entity). Also it, itself, will be able to grow by the stimulations from the outside world. So, it is very important to know the mechanisms of the growing and the whole connections for the growing.

3.   What are the key and the core terms of groups of neurons?

Groups of neurons will be possible to contain the abstracted concept (for example; good, bad, like, dislike, love, affection, reflection, etc.). Those are kinds of artificial entities? Or what?

4.   What is love? How is it created? And how is it matured? What are the mechanism and the connection in the prefrontal cortex?

If the group of neurons in a child's prefrontal cortex of brain that are only positively responding (positive; good matters, hurt nothings, do things without rewards, giving matters to anybody, voluntarily intentions, etc. which will be cored somewhere in the prefrontal cortex), will it become a kind of artificial entity?

5.   What is concurrency? How can the concurrency space be made at the place where the five senses and the neurons information from the cerebellum will be meeting in the computer system?
6.   What is abstract in a sense of neurons' activities?
7.   What is reflection? What sorts of meanings does brain have?
8.   What is reflection in a sense of neuron mechanisms?
9.   What is reflection in a sense of neuron processing?

10. The neuron information which flows from the cerebellum will move into the prefrontal cortex. Is there any definite key mechanism which the neuron information flow moves to under this flow route? This is related with reflection process.

Related Readings

To continue IGI Global's long-standing tradition of advancing innovation through emerging research, please find below a compiled list of recommended IGI Global book chapters and journal articles in the areas of artificial intelligence, human cognition, and human behavior. These related readings will provide additional information and guidance to further enrich your knowledge and assist you with your own research.

Abdolshah, M., Farazmand, N., Mollaaghamirzaei, A., Eshragh, F., & Nezhad, K. G. (2017). Analyzing and Studying the Selection Tests based on their Capabilities in Evaluation of Various Jobs Proficiencies and Abilities. In A. Bhattacharya (Ed.), *Strategic Human Capital Development and Management in Emerging Economies* (pp. 90–109). Hershey, PA: IGI Global. doi:10.4018/978-1-5225-1974-4.ch005

Abuljadail, M. H., Ha, L., Wang, F., & Yang, L. (2015). What Motivates Online Shoppers to "Like" Brands' Facebook Fan Pages? In A. Mesquita & C. Tsai (Eds.), *Human Behavior, Psychology, and Social Interaction in the Digital Era* (pp. 279–293). Hershey, PA: IGI Global. doi:10.4018/978-1-4666-8450-8.ch014

Akbar, S., & Khurana, H. (2017). Chronic Mental Illness in Old Age Homes: An International Perspective. In B. Prasad (Ed.), *Chronic Mental Illness and the Changing Scope of Intervention Strategies, Diagnosis, and Treatment* (pp. 21–39). Hershey, PA: IGI Global. doi:10.4018/978-1-5225-0519-8.ch002

Alcántara-Pilar, J. M., del Barrio-García, S., Crespo-Almendros, E., & Porcu, L. (2015). A Review of Psycho- vs. Socio-Linguistics Theories: An Application to Marketing Research. In J. Alcántara-Pilar, S. del Barrio-García, E. Crespo-Almendros, & L. Porcu (Eds.), *Analyzing the Cultural Diversity of Consumers in the Global Marketplace* (pp. 227–255). Hershey, PA: IGI Global. doi:10.4018/978-1-4666-8262-7.ch011

Alcántara-Pilar, J. M., del Barrio-García, S., Crespo-Almendros, E., & Porcu, L. (2015). The Moderating Role of Language on Perceived Risk and Information-Processing Online. In J. Alcántara-Pilar, S. del Barrio-García, E. Crespo-Almendros, & L. Porcu (Eds.), *Analyzing the Cultural Diversity of Consumers in the Global Marketplace* (pp. 320–345). Hershey, PA: IGI Global. doi:10.4018/978-1-4666-8262-7.ch015

Antonietti, A., Caravita, S. C., Colombo, B., & Simonelli, L. (2015). Blogs' Potentialities in Learning: What Are the Key Variables to Promote Cognitive Empowerment. In A. Mesquita & C. Tsai (Eds.), *Human Behavior, Psychology, and Social Interaction in the Digital Era* (pp. 21–44). Hershey, PA: IGI Global. doi:10.4018/978-1-4666-8450-8.ch002

Antonova, A. (2015). How Social Factors Influence Implicit Knowledge Construction on the Internet. In Z. Jin (Ed.), *Exploring Implicit Cognition: Learning, Memory, and Social Cognitive Processes* (pp. 205–215). Hershey, PA: IGI Global. doi:10.4018/978-1-4666-6599-6.ch010

Araujo, B. H., & Nasseh, I. E. (2017). Understanding the Interdisciplinary Meaning of Beauty to Neuroscience: Designing Beauty to Neuroscience. In R. Zuanon (Ed.), *Projective Processes and Neuroscience in Art and Design* (pp. 103–118). Hershey, PA: IGI Global. doi:10.4018/978-1-5225-0510-5.ch007

Athota, V. S. (2017). Foundations and Future of Well-Being: How Personality Influences Happiness and Well-Being. In S. Háša & R. Brunet-Thornton (Eds.), *Impact of Organizational Trauma on Workplace Behavior and Performance* (pp. 279–294). Hershey, PA: IGI Global. doi:10.4018/978-1-5225-2021-4.ch012

B. N. R., Prasad, B. V., & Tavaragi, M. S. (2017). Legal Aspects of Chronic Mental Illness. In B. Prasad (Ed.), Chronic Mental Illness and the Changing Scope of Intervention Strategies, Diagnosis, and Treatment (pp. 225-235). Hershey, PA: IGI Global. doi:10.4018/978-1-5225-0519-8.ch012

Bandy, J. (2017). Employee Wellness Programs: An International Examination. In F. Topor (Ed.), *Handbook of Research on Individualism and Identity in the Globalized Digital Age* (pp. 359–379). Hershey, PA: IGI Global. doi:10.4018/978-1-5225-0522-8.ch016

Barone, P. A. (2017). Defining and Understanding the Development of Juvenile Delinquency from an Environmental, Sociological, and Theoretical Perspective. In S. Egharevba (Ed.), *Police Brutality, Racial Profiling, and Discrimination in the Criminal Justice System* (pp. 215–238). Hershey, PA: IGI Global. doi:10.4018/978-1-5225-1088-8.ch010

Barratt, J., & Bishop, J. (2015). The Impacts of Alcohol on E-Dating Activity: Increases in Flame Trolling Corresponds with Higher Alcohol Consumption. In J. Bishop (Ed.), *Psychological and Social Implications Surrounding Internet and Gaming Addiction* (pp. 186–197). Hershey, PA: IGI Global. doi:10.4018/978-1-4666-8595-6.ch011

Beard, R. L., & O'Connor, M. K. (2015). Listening to Alzheimer's: The Role of Social Location in Illness Narratives. In C. Dick-Muehlke, R. Li, & M. Orleans (Eds.), *Psychosocial Studies of the Individual's Changing Perspectives in Alzheimer's Disease* (pp. 1–32). Hershey, PA: IGI Global. doi:10.4018/978-1-4666-8478-2.ch001

Bedi, D. (2017). Efficacy of Art Therapy in Treating Patients with Paranoid Schizophrenia. In B. Prasad (Ed.), *Chronic Mental Illness and the Changing Scope of Intervention Strategies, Diagnosis, and Treatment* (pp. 308–320). Hershey, PA: IGI Global. doi:10.4018/978-1-5225-0519-8.ch017

Bermeitinger, C. (2015). Priming. In Z. Jin (Ed.), *Exploring Implicit Cognition: Learning, Memory, and Social Cognitive Processes* (pp. 16–60). Hershey, PA: IGI Global. doi:10.4018/978-1-4666-6599-6.ch002

Bishop, J. (2015). Determining the Risk of Digital Addiction to Adolescent Targets of Internet Trolling: Implications for the UK Legal System. In J. Bishop (Ed.), *Psychological and Social Implications Surrounding Internet and Gaming Addiction* (pp. 31–42). Hershey, PA: IGI Global. doi:10.4018/978-1-4666-8595-6.ch003

Bishop, J. (2015). Using "On-the-Fly Corpus Linguistics" to Systematically Derive Word Definitions Using Inductive Abstraction and Reductionist Correlation Analysis: Considering Seductive and Gratifying Properties of Computer Jargon. In J. Bishop (Ed.), *Psychological and Social Implications Surrounding Internet and Gaming Addiction* (pp. 153–170). Hershey, PA: IGI Global. doi:10.4018/978-1-4666-8595-6.ch009

Boesch, B. (2017). Enabling Creativity: Using Garden Exploration as a Vehicle for Creative Expression and Analysis. In N. Silton (Ed.), *Exploring the Benefits of Creativity in Education, Media, and the Arts* (pp. 117–135). Hershey, PA: IGI Global. doi:10.4018/978-1-5225-0504-4.ch006

Bozoglan, B., & Demirer, V. (2015). The Association between Internet Addiction and Psychosocial Variables. In J. Bishop (Ed.), *Psychological and Social Implications Surrounding Internet and Gaming Addiction* (pp. 171–185). Hershey, PA: IGI Global. doi:10.4018/978-1-4666-8595-6.ch010

Byrd-Poller, L., Farmer, J. L., & Ford, V. (2017). The Role of Leaders in Facilitating Healing After Organizational Trauma. In S. Háša & R. Brunet-Thornton (Eds.), *Impact of Organizational Trauma on Workplace Behavior and Performance* (pp. 318–340). Hershey, PA: IGI Global. doi:10.4018/978-1-5225-2021-4.ch014

Cacho-Elizondo, S., Shahidi, N., & Tossan, V. (2015). Giving Up Smoking Using SMS Messages on your Mobile Phone. In A. Mesquita & C. Tsai (Eds.), *Human Behavior, Psychology, and Social Interaction in the Digital Era* (pp. 72–94). Hershey, PA: IGI Global. doi:10.4018/978-1-4666-8450-8.ch004

Card, S., & Wang, H. (2015). Taking Care to Play: Meaningful Communication in Dementia Care in Chinese Culture. In C. Dick-Muehlke, R. Li, & M. Orleans (Eds.), *Psychosocial Studies of the Individual's Changing Perspectives in Alzheimer's Disease* (pp. 76–103). Hershey, PA: IGI Global. doi:10.4018/978-1-4666-8478-2.ch004

Carrasco, G., & Kinnamon, E. (2017). An Examination of Selfish and Selfless Motives: A Review of the Social Psychological and Behavioral Economics Literature. In R. Ianole (Ed.), *Applied Behavioral Economics Research and Trends* (pp. 93–109). Hershey, PA: IGI Global. doi:10.4018/978-1-5225-1826-6.ch006

Cejka, P., & Mohelska, H. (2017). National Culture Influence on Organisational Trauma: A Conceptual Framework Review. In S. Háša & R. Brunet-Thornton (Eds.), *Impact of Organizational Trauma on Workplace Behavior and Performance* (pp. 162–186). Hershey, PA: IGI Global. doi:10.4018/978-1-5225-2021-4.ch007

Chen, R., Lin, T., & Xie, T. (2015). Towards Intelligent Window Layout Management: The Role of Mental Map. In A. Mesquita & C. Tsai (Eds.), *Human Behavior, Psychology, and Social Interaction in the Digital Era* (pp. 146–161). Hershey, PA: IGI Global. doi:10.4018/978-1-4666-8450-8.ch007

Chuang, S., Lin, S., Chang, T., & Kaewmeesri, R. (2017). Behavioral Intention of Using Social Networking Site: A Comparative Study of Taiwanese and Thai Facebook Users. *International Journal of Technology and Human Interaction*, *13*(1), 61–81. doi:10.4018/IJTHI.2017010104

Cialdella, V. T., Lobato, E. J., & Jordan, J. S. (2017). Wild Architecture: Explaining Cognition via Self-Sustaining Systems. In J. Vallverdú, M. Mazzara, M. Talanov, S. Distefano, & R. Lowe (Eds.), *Advanced Research on Biologically Inspired Cognitive Architectures* (pp. 41–62). Hershey, PA: IGI Global. doi:10.4018/978-1-5225-1947-8.ch003

Cleve, R. A., Işık, İ., & Pecanha, V. D. (2017). Sexual Identities in the Workplace: Avoiding Organizational Trauma When Disclosure Occurs – Current Perspectives. In S. Háša & R. Brunet-Thornton (Eds.), *Impact of Organizational Trauma on Workplace Behavior and Performance* (pp. 188–220). Hershey, PA: IGI Global. doi:10.4018/978-1-5225-2021-4.ch008

Contier, A. T., & Torres, L. (2017). Neuroaesthetics: Insights into the Aesthetic Experience of Visual Art. In R. Zuanon (Ed.), *Projective Processes and Neuroscience in Art and Design* (pp. 87–102). Hershey, PA: IGI Global. doi:10.4018/978-1-5225-0510-5.ch006

Crawford, C. M., & Smith, M. S. (2015). Rethinking Bloom's Taxonomy: Implicit Cognitive Vulnerability as an Impetus towards Higher Order Thinking Skills. In Z. Jin (Ed.), *Exploring Implicit Cognition: Learning, Memory, and Social Cognitive Processes* (pp. 86–103). Hershey, PA: IGI Global. doi:10.4018/978-1-4666-6599-6.ch004 de Soir, E., & Kleber, R. (2017). Understanding the Core of Psychological Trauma: Trauma in Contemporary French Theory. In S. Háša & R. Brunet-Thornton (Eds.), *Impact of Organizational Trauma on Workplace Behavior and Performance* (pp. 57–75). Hershey, PA: IGI Global. doi:10.4018/978-1-5225-2021-4.ch003

Delgado, J. J. (2017). How Is the Personality of Facebook Customers?: Cloninger's Psychobiological Model of Temperament as a Predictor of SNSs. In M. Dos Santos (Ed.), *Applying Neuroscience to Business Practice* (pp. 191–229). Hershey, PA: IGI Global. doi:10.4018/978-1-5225-1028-4.ch009

Dentale, F., Vecchione, M., & Barbaranelli, C. (2015). Applying the IAT to Assess Big Five Personality Traits: A Brief Review of Measurement and Validity Issues. In Z. Jin (Ed.), *Exploring Implicit Cognition: Learning, Memory, and Social Cognitive Processes* (pp. 1–15). Hershey, PA: IGI Global. doi:10.4018/978-1-4666-6599-6.ch001

Díez, J. C., & Saiz-Alvarez, J. M. (2016). Leadership in Social Entrepreneurship: Is It Ability or Skill? In J. Saiz-Álvarez (Ed.), *Handbook of Research on Social Entrepreneurship and Solidarity Economics* (pp. 134–153). Hershey, PA: IGI Global. doi:10.4018/978-1-5225-0097-1.ch008

Dikici, A. (2017). Revisiting the Relationships between Turkish Prospective Teachers' Thinking Styles and Behaviors Fostering Creativity. In N. Silton (Ed.), *Exploring the Benefits of Creativity in Education, Media, and the Arts* (pp. 136–157). Hershey, PA: IGI Global. doi:10.4018/978-1-5225-0504-4.ch007

Eapen, V., & Walter, A. (2016). Mind the Gap: Developmental Vulnerability and Mental Health. In R. Gopalan (Ed.), *Handbook of Research on Diagnosing, Treating, and Managing Intellectual Disabilities* (pp. 11–32). Hershey, PA: IGI Global. doi:10.4018/978-1-5225-0089-6.ch002

Fallon, F. (2017). Integrated Information Theory (IIT) and Artificial Consciousness. In J. Vallverdú, M. Mazzara, M. Talanov, S. Distefano, & R. Lowe (Eds.), *Advanced Research on Biologically Inspired Cognitive Architectures* (pp. 1–23). Hershey, PA: IGI Global. doi:10.4018/978-1-5225-1947-8.ch001

Fang, L., & Ha, L. (2015). Do College Students Benefit from Their Social Media Experience?: Social Media Involvement and Its Impact on College Students' Self-Efficacy Perception. In A. Mesquita & C. Tsai (Eds.), *Human Behavior, Psychology, and Social Interaction in the Digital Era* (pp. 259–278). Hershey, PA: IGI Global. doi:10.4018/978-1-4666-8450-8.ch013

Fasko, D. (2017). Creativity in the Schools: Educational Changes Lately? In N. Silton (Ed.), *Exploring the Benefits of Creativity in Education, Media, and the Arts* (pp. 92–116). Hershey, PA: IGI Global. doi:10.4018/978-1-5225-0504-4.ch005

Fazio, S., & Mitchell, D. B. (2015). Self-Preservation in Individuals with Alzheimer's Disease: Empirical Evidence and the Role of the Social Environment. In C. Dick-Muehlke, R. Li, & M. Orleans (Eds.), *Psychosocial Studies of the Individual's Changing Perspectives in Alzheimer's Disease* (pp. 183–207). Hershey, PA: IGI Global. doi:10.4018/978-1-4666-8478-2.ch008

Feitosa-Santana, C. (2017). Understanding How the Mind Works: The Neuroscience of Perception, Behavior, and Creativity. In R. Zuanon (Ed.), *Projective Processes and Neuroscience in Art and Design* (pp. 239–252). Hershey, PA: IGI Global. doi:10.4018/978-1-5225-0510-5.ch014

Ferris, A. (2017). Creativity in the Emerging Adult. In N. Silton (Ed.), *Exploring the Benefits of Creativity in Education, Media, and the Arts* (pp. 26–49). Hershey, PA: IGI Global. doi:10.4018/978-1-5225-0504-4.ch002

Fogliano, F., & Oliveira, H. C. (2017). Neuroesthetics: Perspectives and Reflections. In R. Zuanon (Ed.), *Projective Processes and Neuroscience in Art and Design* (pp. 52–70). Hershey, PA: IGI Global. doi:10.4018/978-1-5225-0510-5.ch004

Folk, J. R., & Eskenazi, M. A. (2017). Eye Movement Behavior and Individual Differences in Word Identification During Reading. In C. Was, F. Sansosti, & B. Morris (Eds.), *Eye-Tracking Technology Applications in Educational Research* (pp. 66–87). Hershey, PA: IGI Global. doi:10.4018/978-1-5225-1005-5.ch004

Franco, M., Ortiz, T. V., Amorim, H. A., & Faber, J. (2017). Can We Induce a Cognitive Representation of a Prosthetic Arm by Means of Crossmodal Stimuli? In R. Zuanon (Ed.), *Projective Processes and Neuroscience in Art and Design* (pp. 182–204). Hershey, PA: IGI Global. doi:10.4018/978-1-5225-0510-5.ch011

G., L. (2017). Psychosocial Intervention Studies for Street Children with Substance Abuse. In B. Prasad (Ed.), *Chronic Mental Illness and the Changing Scope of Intervention Strategies, Diagnosis, and Treatment* (pp. 237-257). Hershey, PA: IGI Global. doi:10.4018/978-1-5225-0519-8.ch013

Gallego, J. (2017). Organizational Trauma and Change Management. In S. Háša & R. Brunet-Thornton (Eds.), *Impact of Organizational Trauma on Workplace Behavior and Performance* (pp. 140–161). Hershey, PA: IGI Global. doi:10.4018/978-1-5225-2021-4.ch006

Galvin, J. E., & Kelleher, M. E. (2015). Dementia and Other Neurocognitive Disorders: An Overview. In C. Dick-Muehlke, R. Li, & M. Orleans (Eds.), *Psychosocial Studies of the Individual's Changing Perspectives in Alzheimer's Disease* (pp. 104–130). Hershey, PA: IGI Global. doi:10.4018/978-1-4666-8478-2.ch005

Gardner, M. K., & Strayer, D. L. (2017). What Cognitive Psychology Can Tell Us About Educational Computer Games. In R. Zheng & M. Gardner (Eds.), *Handbook of Research on Serious Games for Educational Applications* (pp. 1–18). Hershey, PA: IGI Global. doi:10.4018/978-1-5225-0513-6.ch001

Garg, B., Khanna, P., & Khanna, A. (2017). Chronic Mental Illness and the Changing Scope of Intervention Strategies, Diagnosis, and Treatment in Child and Adolescent Population. In B. Prasad (Ed.), *Chronic Mental Illness and the Changing Scope of Intervention Strategies, Diagnosis, and Treatment* (pp. 258–269). Hershey, PA: IGI Global. doi:10.4018/978-1-5225-0519-8.ch014

Giannouli, V. (2017). Creativity and Giftedness: A Study of Attitudes. In N. Silton (Ed.), *Exploring the Benefits of Creativity in Education, Media, and the Arts* (pp. 179–197). Hershey, PA: IGI Global. doi:10.4018/978-1-5225-0504-4.ch009

Gopalan, R. T. (2016). Intellectual Disability: From History to Recent Trends. In R. Gopalan (Ed.), *Handbook of Research on Diagnosing, Treating, and Managing Intellectual Disabilities* (pp. 1–10). Hershey, PA: IGI Global. doi:10.4018/978-1-5225-0089-6.ch001

Hacker, D. J. (2017). The Role of Metacognition in Learning via Serious Games. In R. Zheng & M. Gardner (Eds.), *Handbook of Research on Serious Games for Educational Applications* (pp. 19–40). Hershey, PA: IGI Global. doi:10.4018/978-1-5225-0513-6.ch002

Halder, S., & Mahato, A. (2017). Cognitive Remediation Therapy in Chronic Schizophrenia. In B. Prasad (Ed.), *Chronic Mental Illness and the Changing Scope of Intervention Strategies, Diagnosis, and Treatment* (pp. 292–307). Hershey, PA: IGI Global. doi:10.4018/978-1-5225-0519-8.ch016

Heins, S., Heins, G., & Dick-Muehlke, C. (2015). Steve's Story: Living with Mild Cognitive Impairment. In C. Dick-Muehlke, R. Li, & M. Orleans (Eds.), *Psychosocial Studies of the Individual's Changing Perspectives in Alzheimer's Disease* (pp. 33–60). Hershey, PA: IGI Global. doi:10.4018/978-1-4666-8478-2.ch002

Isik, I. (2017). Organizations and Exposure to Trauma at a Collective Level: The Taxonomy of Potentially Traumatic Events. In S. Háša & R. Brunet-Thornton (Eds.), *Impact of Organizational Trauma on Workplace Behavior and Performance* (pp. 18–56). Hershey, PA: IGI Global. doi:10.4018/978-1-5225-2021-4.ch002

Jančec, L., Vorkapić, S. T., & Vodopivec, J. L. (2015). Hidden Curriculum Determinants in (Pre)School Institutions: Implicit Cognition in Action. In Z. Jin (Ed.), *Exploring Implicit Cognition: Learning, Memory, and Social Cognitive Processes* (pp. 216–242). Hershey, PA: IGI Global. doi:10.4018/978-1-4666-6599-6.ch011

Jerabek, I., & Muoio, D. (2017). The Stress Profile: The Influence of Personal Characteristics on Response to Occupational Trauma. In S. Háša & R. Brunet-Thornton (Eds.), *Impact of Organizational Trauma on Workplace Behavior and Performance* (pp. 77–119). Hershey, PA: IGI Global. doi:10.4018/978-1-5225-2021-4.ch004

Jha, S., Khanna, A., & Khanna, P. (2017). Advanced Intervention Strategies for Suicide in Patients with Chronic Mental Illness. In B. Prasad (Ed.), *Chronic Mental Illness and the Changing Scope of Intervention Strategies, Diagnosis, and Treatment* (pp. 271–291). Hershey, PA: IGI Global. doi:10.4018/978-1-5225-0519-8.ch015

Johard, L., Lippi, V., Safina, L., & Mazzara, M. (2017). Mind and Matter: Why It All Makes Sense. In J. Vallverdú, M. Mazzara, M. Talanov, S. Distefano, & R. Lowe (Eds.), *Advanced Research on Biologically Inspired Cognitive Architectures* (pp. 63–82). Hershey, PA: IGI Global. doi:10.4018/978-1-5225-1947-8.ch004

Kasemsap, K. (2017). Investigating the Roles of Neuroscience and Knowledge Management in Higher Education. In S. Mukerji & P. Tripathi (Eds.), *Handbook of Research on Administration, Policy, and Leadership in Higher Education* (pp. 112–140). Hershey, PA: IGI Global. doi:10.4018/978-1-5225-0672-0.ch006

Kasemsap, K. (2017). Mastering Cognitive Neuroscience and Social Neuroscience Perspectives in the Information Age. In M. Dos Santos (Ed.), *Applying Neuroscience to Business Practice* (pp. 82–113). Hershey, PA: IGI Global. doi:10.4018/978-1-5225-1028-4.ch005

Kaushik, P., & Singh, T. B. (2017). Predictors of Expressed Emotion, Caregiver's Burden, and Quality of Life in Chronic Mental Illness. In B. Prasad (Ed.), *Chronic Mental Illness and the Changing Scope of Intervention Strategies, Diagnosis, and Treatment* (pp. 143–163). Hershey, PA: IGI Global. doi:10.4018/978-1-5225-0519-8.ch008

Keyser, A. K., & Corning, M. (2017). Creative Aging: Stimulating Creativity in Middle and Late Adulthood. In N. Silton (Ed.), *Exploring the Benefits of Creativity in Education, Media, and the Arts* (pp. 50–66). Hershey, PA: IGI Global. doi:10.4018/978-1-5225-0504-4.ch003

Kılıç, B. (2017). An Organizational Trauma Intervention: A Case From Turkey. In S. Háša & R. Brunet-Thornton (Eds.), *Impact of Organizational Trauma on Workplace Behavior and Performance* (pp. 264–277). Hershey, PA: IGI Global. doi:10.4018/978-1-5225-2021-4.ch011

Kirsch, C., Lubart, T., de Vries, H., & Houssemand, C. (2017). Scientific Creativity in Psychology: A Cognitive-Conative Approach. In C. Zhou (Ed.), *Handbook of Research on Creative Problem-Solving Skill Development in Higher Education* (pp. 51–73). Hershey, PA: IGI Global. doi:10.4018/978-1-5225-0643-0.ch003

Kleinmintz, O. M. (2017). Train Yourself to Let Go: The Benefits of Deliberate Practice on Creativity and Its Neural Basis. In N. Silton (Ed.), *Exploring the Benefits of Creativity in Education, Media, and the Arts* (pp. 67–90). Hershey, PA: IGI Global. doi:10.4018/978-1-5225-0504-4.ch004

Kučera, D. (2017). The Potential of Spirituality for the Treatment of Organizational Trauma. In S. Háša & R. Brunet-Thornton (Eds.), *Impact of Organizational Trauma on Workplace Behavior and Performance* (pp. 295–317). Hershey, PA: IGI Global. doi:10.4018/978-1-5225-2021-4.ch013

Kukreti, P., Khanna, P., & Khanna, A. (2017). Chronic Mental Illnesses and Homelessness. In B. Prasad (Ed.), *Chronic Mental Illness and the Changing Scope of Intervention Strategies, Diagnosis, and Treatment* (pp. 1–20). Hershey, PA: IGI Global. doi:10.4018/978-1-5225-0519-8.ch001

Kuss, D. J. (2015). "I Can't Do It by Myself": An IPA of Clients Seeking Psychotherapy for Their MMORPG Addiction. In J. Bishop (Ed.), *Psychological and Social Implications Surrounding Internet and Gaming Addiction* (pp. 78–110). Hershey, PA: IGI Global. doi:10.4018/978-1-4666-8595-6.ch006

Landim, P. D. (2017). Design and Emotion: Contributions to the Emotional Design. In R. Zuanon (Ed.), *Projective Processes and Neuroscience in Art and Design* (pp. 119–136). Hershey, PA: IGI Global. doi:10.4018/978-1-5225-0510-5.ch008

Lebraty, J., & Godé, C. (2015). Assessing the Performance of Decision Support Systems in Military Environment: The 3C Method. In A. Mesquita & C. Tsai (Eds.), *Human Behavior, Psychology, and Social Interaction in the Digital Era* (pp. 45–70). Hershey, PA: IGI Global. doi:10.4018/978-1-4666-8450-8.ch003

Lehenbauer-Baum, M., & Fohringer, M. (2015). Internet Gaming Disorder: A Deeper Look into Addiction vs. High Engagement. In J. Bishop (Ed.), *Psychological and Social Implications Surrounding Internet and Gaming Addiction* (pp. 1–15). Hershey, PA: IGI Global. doi:10.4018/978-1-4666-8595-6.ch001

Lei, M., Liu, W., Gao, Y., & Zhu, T. (2015). Mobile User Behaviors in China. In Z. Yan (Ed.), *Encyclopedia of Mobile Phone Behavior* (pp. 1110–1128). Hershey, PA: IGI Global. doi:10.4018/978-1-4666-8239-9.ch091

Leote, R. (2017). Perceptual Processes and Multisensoriality: Understanding Multimodal Art from Neuroscientific Concepts. In R. Zuanon (Ed.), *Projective Processes and Neuroscience in Art and Design* (pp. 1–14). Hershey, PA: IGI Global. doi:10.4018/978-1-5225-0510-5.ch001

Lin, L., & Lipsmeyer, B. (2015). The Environmental and Technological Factors of Multitasking. In A. Mesquita & C. Tsai (Eds.), *Human Behavior, Psychology, and Social Interaction in the Digital Era* (pp. 1–20). Hershey, PA: IGI Global. doi:10.4018/978-1-4666-8450-8.ch001

Lin, T., Wu, Z., & Chen, Y. (2015). Using High-Frequency Interaction Events to Automatically Classify Cognitive Load. In A. Mesquita & C. Tsai (Eds.), *Human Behavior, Psychology, and Social Interaction in the Digital Era* (pp. 210–228). Hershey, PA: IGI Global. doi:10.4018/978-1-4666-8450-8.ch010

Liu, X., & Zhu, T. (2017). Comparing Online Personality of Americans and Chinese. In I. Management Association (Ed.), Gaming and Technology Addiction: Breakthroughs in Research and Practice (pp. 339-351). Hershey, PA: IGI Global. doi:10.4018/978-1-5225-0778-9.ch016

Lopes, M. M. (2017). Inside/Out: Looking Back into the Future. In R. Zuanon (Ed.), *Projective Processes and Neuroscience in Art and Design* (pp. 15–39). Hershey, PA: IGI Global. doi:10.4018/978-1-5225-0510-5.ch002

Lu, Y. Y., & Austrom, M. G. (2015). Disease Awareness, Cognitive Decline, and Communication in Persons with Mild Cognitive Impairment and Caregivers. In C. Dick-Muehlke, R. Li, & M. Orleans (Eds.), *Psychosocial Studies of the Individual's Changing Perspectives in Alzheimer's Disease* (pp. 254–270). Hershey, PA: IGI Global. doi:10.4018/978-1-4666-8478-2.ch011

Lytras, M. D., Raghavan, V., & Damiani, E. (2017). Big Data and Data Analytics Research: From Metaphors to Value Space for Collective Wisdom in Human Decision Making and Smart Machines. *International Journal on Semantic Web and Information Systems*, *13*(1), 1–10. doi:10.4018/IJSWIS.2017010101

M., K., & Boominathan, P. (2016). Assessment and Management of Communication Skills in Individuals with Intellectual Disability: Perspectives in the 21st Century. In R. Gopalan (Ed.), *Handbook of Research on Diagnosing, Treating, and Managing Intellectual Disabilities* (pp. 156-185). Hershey, PA: IGI Global. doi:10.4018/978-1-5225-0089-6.ch009

MacKinlay, E., & Trevitt, C. (2015). Spiritual Factors in the Experience of Alzheimer's Disease and Other Dementias. In C. Dick-Muehlke, R. Li, & M. Orleans (Eds.), *Psychosocial Studies of the Individual's Changing Perspectives in Alzheimer's Disease* (pp. 230–253). Hershey, PA: IGI Global. doi:10.4018/978-1-4666-8478-2.ch010

Mahato, A., & Halder, S. (2017). Disability in Schizophrenia: The Psychosocial and Neurocognitive Perspective. In B. Prasad (Ed.), *Chronic Mental Illness and the Changing Scope of Intervention Strategies, Diagnosis, and Treatment* (pp. 188–202). Hershey, PA: IGI Global. doi:10.4018/978-1-5225-0519-8.ch010

Manthiou, A., Chiang, L. L., & Tang, L. R. (2015). Developing a Successful Facebook Fan Page Based on Costumers' Needs. In A. Mesquita & C. Tsai (Eds.), *Human Behavior, Psychology, and Social Interaction in the Digital Era* (pp. 189–209). Hershey, PA: IGI Global. doi:10.4018/978-1-4666-8450-8.ch009

McCutcheon, J. L. (2017). Emerging Ethical Issues in Police and Public Safety Psychology: Reflections on Mandatory vs. Aspirational Ethics. In C. Mitchell & E. Dorian (Eds.), *Police Psychology and Its Growing Impact on Modern Law Enforcement* (pp. 314–334). Hershey, PA: IGI Global. doi:10.4018/978-1-5225-0813-7.ch016

Menezes, M. (2017). Cells, Organisms, and the Living Brain as New Media for Art: A Pursuit in Art Research. In R. Zuanon (Ed.), *Projective Processes and Neuroscience in Art and Design* (pp. 40–50). Hershey, PA: IGI Global. doi:10.4018/978-1-5225-0510-5.ch003

Mitchell, C. L. (2017). Preemployment Psychological Screening of Police Officer Applicants: Basic Considerations and Recent Advances. In C. Mitchell & E. Dorian (Eds.), *Police Psychology and Its Growing Impact on Modern Law Enforcement* (pp. 28–50). Hershey, PA: IGI Global. doi:10.4018/978-1-5225-0813-7.ch002

Mittlböck, K. (2015). Dangers of Playing with the Virtual Other in Mind: A Psychoanalytical View on Digital Role-Playing Games and the Edge between Facilitating Personality Development and Endangering the Player's Psyche. In J. Bishop (Ed.), *Psychological and Social Implications Surrounding Internet and Gaming Addiction* (pp. 44–61). Hershey, PA: IGI Global. doi:10.4018/978-1-4666-8595-6.ch004

Moraru, A. (2017). Student's Psychological Factors and Metacognitive Skills in Higher Education. In E. Railean, A. Elçi, & A. Elçi (Eds.), *Metacognition and Successful Learning Strategies in Higher Education* (pp. 176–199). Hershey, PA: IGI Global. doi:10.4018/978-1-5225-2218-8.ch009

Morhardt, D., & Spira, M. (2015). Cognitive Decline and the Changing Self in Relationship. In C. Dick-Muehlke, R. Li, & M. Orleans (Eds.), *Psychosocial Studies of the Individual's Changing Perspectives in Alzheimer's Disease* (pp. 61–75). Hershey, PA: IGI Global. doi:10.4018/978-1-4666-8478-2.ch003

Nakamura, D. (2015). Individual Differences in Implicit Learning: Current Problems and Issues for Research. In Z. Jin (Ed.), *Exploring Implicit Cognition: Learning, Memory, and Social Cognitive Processes* (pp. 61–85). Hershey, PA: IGI Global. doi:10.4018/978-1-4666-6599-6.ch003

Navarro, A. B., Díaz-Orueta, U., Martín-Niño, L., & Sánchez-Sánchez, M. E. (2015). Art, Drawing Task Processes, and Identity Awareness: A Case Study on the Retro-Genesis Phenomenon as an Indicator of the Progress of Dementia. In C. Dick-Muehlke, R. Li, & M. Orleans (Eds.), *Psychosocial Studies of the Individual's Changing Perspectives in Alzheimer's Disease* (pp. 208–228). Hershey, PA: IGI Global. doi:10.4018/978-1-4666-8478-2.ch009

Nina, B., & Nadejda, B. (2017). Metacognitive Strategies in Higher Education: Development of Spiritual Intelligence Strategies Within Training of the Academic Staff. In E. Railean, A. Elçi, & A. Elçi (Eds.), *Metacognition and Successful Learning Strategies in Higher Education* (pp. 109–136). Hershey, PA: IGI Global. doi:10.4018/978-1-5225-2218-8.ch006

Norris, S. E., & Porter, T. H. (2017). The Influence of Spirituality in the Workplace and Perceived Organizational Support on Organizational Citizenship Behaviors for Strategic Success. In V. Wang (Ed.), *Encyclopedia of Strategic Leadership and Management* (pp. 1140–1162). Hershey, PA: IGI Global. doi:10.4018/978-1-5225-1049-9.ch080

O'Reilly, A. G., Roche, B., & Cartwright, A. (2015). Function over Form: A Behavioral Approach to Implicit Attitudes. In Z. Jin (Ed.), *Exploring Implicit Cognition: Learning, Memory, and Social Cognitive Processes* (pp. 162–182). Hershey, PA: IGI Global. doi:10.4018/978-1-4666-6599-6.ch008

Pandey, J. M., Mishra, P., Garg, S., & Mshra, B. P. (2017). Chronic Mental Illness and Dumping Patients: A Concern towards Management. In B. Prasad (Ed.), *Chronic Mental Illness and the Changing Scope of Intervention Strategies, Diagnosis, and Treatment* (pp. 40–57). Hershey, PA: IGI Global. doi:10.4018/978-1-5225-0519-8.ch003

Pantos, A. J. (2015). Implicit Social Cognition and Language Attitudes Research. In Z. Jin (Ed.), *Exploring Implicit Cognition: Learning, Memory, and Social Cognitive Processes* (pp. 104–117). Hershey, PA: IGI Global. doi:10.4018/978-1-4666-6599-6.ch005

Park, L. Q., & Busson, B. (2015). The Impact of Decline on Everyday Life in Alzheimer's Disease. In C. Dick-Muehlke, R. Li, & M. Orleans (Eds.), *Psychosocial Studies of the Individual's Changing Perspectives in Alzheimer's Disease* (pp. 327–338). Hershey, PA: IGI Global. doi:10.4018/978-1-4666-8478-2.ch014

Pellas, N. (2015). Unraveling a Progressive Inquiry Script in Persistent Virtual Worlds: Theoretical Foundations and Decision Processes for Constructing a Socio-Cultural Learning Framework. In Z. Jin (Ed.), *Exploring Implicit Cognition: Learning, Memory, and Social Cognitive Processes* (pp. 243–280). Hershey, PA: IGI Global. doi:10.4018/978-1-4666-6599-6.ch012

Pena, P. A., Van den Broucke, S., Sylin, M., Leysen, J., & de Soir, E. (2017). Definitions, Typologies, and Processes Involved in Organizational Trauma: A Literature Review. In S. Háša & R. Brunet-Thornton (Eds.), *Impact of Organizational Trauma on Workplace Behavior and Performance* (pp. 1–17). Hershey, PA: IGI Global. doi:10.4018/978-1-5225-2021-4.ch001

Photiadis, T., & Souleles, N. (2015). A Theoretical Model, Including User-Experience, Aesthetics, and Psychology, in the 3D Design Process. In J. Bishop (Ed.), *Psychological and Social Implications Surrounding Internet and Gaming Addiction* (pp. 139–152). Hershey, PA: IGI Global. doi:10.4018/978-1-4666-8595-6.ch008

Pontes, H. M., & Griffiths, M. D. (2015). New Concepts, Old Known Issues: The DSM-5 and Internet Gaming Disorder and its Assessment. In J. Bishop (Ed.), *Psychological and Social Implications Surrounding Internet and Gaming Addiction* (pp. 16–30). Hershey, PA: IGI Global. doi:10.4018/978-1-4666-8595-6.ch002

Power, G. A. (2015). Changing Perception in Alzheimer's: An Experiential View. In C. Dick-Muehlke, R. Li, & M. Orleans (Eds.), *Psychosocial Studies of the Individual's Changing Perspectives in Alzheimer's Disease* (pp. 271–300). Hershey, PA: IGI Global. doi:10.4018/978-1-4666-8478-2.ch012

R., A., Prasad, B. V., & Kosgi, S. (2017). Psychosocial Intervention Strategies for Patients with Schizophrenia: In Chronic Mental Illness. In B. Prasad (Ed.), *Chronic Mental Illness and the Changing Scope of Intervention Strategies, Diagnosis, and Treatment* (pp. 58-75). Hershey, PA: IGI Global. doi:10.4018/978-1-5225-0519-8.ch004

Reinert, L. (2017). Qualia and Extended Field of Contemporary Design. In R. Zuanon (Ed.), *Projective Processes and Neuroscience in Art and Design* (pp. 138–154). Hershey, PA: IGI Global. doi:10.4018/978-1-5225-0510-5.ch009

Ross, D. B., Exposito, J. A., & Kennedy, T. (2017). Stress and Its Relationship to Leadership and a Healthy Workplace Culture. In V. Bryan & J. Bird (Eds.), *Healthcare Community Synergism between Patients, Practitioners, and Researchers* (pp. 213–246). Hershey, PA: IGI Global. doi:10.4018/978-1-5225-0640-9.ch010

Saberi, M. (2016). Personality-Based Cognitive Design of Characters in Virtual Environments. In J. Turner, M. Nixon, U. Bernardet, & S. DiPaola (Eds.), *Integrating Cognitive Architectures into Virtual Character Design* (pp. 124–150). Hershey, PA: IGI Global. doi:10.4018/978-1-5225-0454-2.ch005

Sharma, R., & Lohan, A. (2016). Psychosocial Interventions for Individuals with Intellectual Disability. In R. Gopalan (Ed.), *Handbook of Research on Diagnosing, Treating, and Managing Intellectual Disabilities* (pp. 262–282). Hershey, PA: IGI Global. doi:10.4018/978-1-5225-0089-6.ch014

Sharon, D. (2015). The Sleep-Wake System and Alzheimer's Disease. In C. Dick-Muehlke, R. Li, & M. Orleans (Eds.), *Psychosocial Studies of the Individual's Changing Perspectives in Alzheimer's Disease* (pp. 339–365). Hershey, PA: IGI Global. doi:10.4018/978-1-4666-8478-2.ch015

Simuth, J. (2017). Psychological Impacts of Downsizing Trauma. In S. Háša & R. Brunet-Thornton (Eds.), *Impact of Organizational Trauma on Workplace Behavior and Performance* (pp. 120–139). Hershey, PA: IGI Global. doi:10.4018/978-1-5225-2021-4.ch005

Sinha, P., Garg, A., Khanna, P., & Khanna, A. (2017). Management of Chronic Mental Illnesses and Substance Use Disorders. In B. Prasad (Ed.), *Chronic Mental Illness and the Changing Scope of Intervention Strategies, Diagnosis, and Treatment* (pp. 101–122). Hershey, PA: IGI Global. doi:10.4018/978-1-5225-0519-8.ch006

Siqueira de Freitas, A. (2017). A Study on the Interface between Arts and Sciences: Neuroesthetics and Cognitive Neuroscience of Art. In R. Zuanon (Ed.), *Projective Processes and Neuroscience in Art and Design* (pp. 71–86). Hershey, PA: IGI Global. doi:10.4018/978-1-5225-0510-5.ch005

Solo, A. M., & Bishop, J. (2015). Avoiding Adverse Consequences from Digital Addiction and Retaliatory Feedback: The Role of the Participation Continuum. In J. Bishop (Ed.), *Psychological and Social Implications Surrounding Internet and Gaming Addiction* (pp. 62–77). Hershey, PA: IGI Global. doi:10.4018/978-1-4666-8595-6.ch005

Soni, S. C. P., & Ahamed, P. C. (2017). Understanding and Management of Caregivers' Stress and Burden of Person with Obsessive Compulsive Disorder. In B. Prasad (Ed.), *Chronic Mental Illness and the Changing Scope of Intervention Strategies, Diagnosis, and Treatment* (pp. 124–142). Hershey, PA: IGI Global. doi:10.4018/978-1-5225-0519-8.ch007

Srivastav, D., & Singh, T. B. (2017). Comorbidity Issues and Treatment in Chronic Mental Illness. In B. Prasad (Ed.), *Chronic Mental Illness and the Changing Scope of Intervention Strategies, Diagnosis, and Treatment* (pp. 77–100). Hershey, PA: IGI Global. doi:10.4018/978-1-5225-0519-8.ch005

Strang, K. D. (2017). Predicting Student Satisfaction and Outcomes in Online Courses Using Learning Activity Indicators. *International Journal of Web-Based Learning and Teaching Technologies, 12*(1), 32–50. doi:10.4018/IJWLTT.2017010103

Svanström, R. (2015). Fragmented Existence: Living Alone with Dementia and a Manifest Care Need. In C. Dick-Muehlke, R. Li, & M. Orleans (Eds.), *Psychosocial Studies of the Individual's Changing Perspectives in Alzheimer's Disease* (pp. 302–326). Hershey, PA: IGI Global. doi:10.4018/978-1-4666-8478-2.ch013

Swiatek, L. (2017). Accessing the Finest Minds: Insights into Creativity from Esteemed Media Professionals. In N. Silton (Ed.), *Exploring the Benefits of Creativity in Education, Media, and the Arts* (pp. 240–263). Hershey, PA: IGI Global. doi:10.4018/978-1-5225-0504-4.ch012

Szymanski, M., & Schindler, E. (2017). Embracing Organizational Trauma: Positive Effects of Death Experiences on Organizational Culture – Three Short Case Studies. In S. Háša & R. Brunet-Thornton (Eds.), *Impact of Organizational Trauma on Workplace Behavior and Performance* (pp. 247–263). Hershey, PA: IGI Global. doi:10.4018/978-1-5225-2021-4.ch010

Tavaragi, M. S. (2017). Chronic Mental Illness in Prisons: Global Scenario. In B. Prasad (Ed.), *Chronic Mental Illness and the Changing Scope of Intervention Strategies, Diagnosis, and Treatment* (pp. 203–224). Hershey, PA: IGI Global. doi:10.4018/978-1-5225-0519-8.ch011

Tavaragi, M. S., & C., S. (2017). Global Burden of Mental Disorders: Quality of Care and Unmet Needs for Treatment of Chronic Mental Illness. In B. Prasad (Ed.), *Chronic Mental Illness and the Changing Scope of Intervention Strategies, Diagnosis, and Treatment* (pp. 164-186). Hershey, PA: IGI Global. doi:10.4018/978-1-5225-0519-8.ch009

Tietze, R. L. (2017). Creativity and the Arts. In N. Silton (Ed.), *Exploring the Benefits of Creativity in Education, Media, and the Arts* (pp. 337–375). Hershey, PA: IGI Global. doi:10.4018/978-1-5225-0504-4.ch016

Toms, G., Lawrence, C., & Clare, L. (2015). Awareness, Self, and the Experience of Dementia: Foundations of a Psychologically Minded Approach. In C. Dick-Muehlke, R. Li, & M. Orleans (Eds.), *Psychosocial Studies of the Individual's Changing Perspectives in Alzheimer's Disease* (pp. 132–158). Hershey, PA: IGI Global. doi:10.4018/978-1-4666-8478-2.ch006

Tran, B. (2017). Impact of Organizational Trauma on Workplace Behavior and Performance: Workplace Bullying Due to (In)Competency. In S. Háša, & R. Brunet-Thornton (Eds.), Impact of Organizational Trauma on Workplace Behavior and Performance (pp. 221-245). Hershey, PA: IGI Global. doi:10.4018/978-1-5225-2021-4.ch009

Tran, B. (2017). Psychological (and Emotional) Architecture: The Values and Benefits of Nature-Based Architecture – Biophilia. In G. Koç, M. Claes, & B. Christiansen (Eds.), *Cultural Influences on Architecture* (pp. 200–230). Hershey, PA: IGI Global. doi:10.4018/978-1-5225-1744-3.ch008

Tran, B. (2017). The Architect of Organizational Psychology: The Geert Hofstede's Dimensions of Cultural (Corporate and Organizational) Identity. In G. Koç, M. Claes, & B. Christiansen (Eds.), *Cultural Influences on Architecture* (pp. 231–258). Hershey, PA: IGI Global. doi:10.4018/978-1-5225-1744-3.ch009

Triberti, S., & Chirico, A. (2017). Healthy Avatars, Healthy People: Care Engagement Through the Shared Experience of Virtual Worlds. In G. Graffigna (Ed.), *Transformative Healthcare Practice through Patient Engagement* (pp. 247–275). Hershey, PA: IGI Global. doi:10.4018/978-1-5225-0663-8.ch010

Tripathi, M. A., & Sridevi, G. (2017). Psychotherapeutic Interventions in Emotional and Behavioural Problems with Adolescents. In B. Prasad (Ed.), *Chronic Mental Illness and the Changing Scope of Intervention Strategies, Diagnosis, and Treatment* (pp. 321–333). Hershey, PA: IGI Global. doi:10.4018/978-1-5225-0519-8.ch018

Trompetter, P. S. (2017). A History of Police Psychology. In C. Mitchell & E. Dorian (Eds.), *Police Psychology and Its Growing Impact on Modern Law Enforcement* (pp. 1–26). Hershey, PA: IGI Global. doi:10.4018/978-1-5225-0813-7.ch001

Valencia, E. (2017). Neuromarketing Step by Step: Based on Scientific Publications. In M. Dos Santos (Ed.), *Applying Neuroscience to Business Practice* (pp. 18–48). Hershey, PA: IGI Global. doi:10.4018/978-1-5225-1028-4.ch002

Valeyeva, N. S., Kupriyanov, R., & Valeyeva, E. R. (2017). Metacognition and Metacognitive Skills: Intellectual Skills Development Technology. In E. Railean, A. Elçi, & A. Elçi (Eds.), *Metacognition and Successful Learning Strategies in Higher Education* (pp. 63–84). Hershey, PA: IGI Global. doi:10.4018/978-1-5225-2218-8.ch004

Vallverdú, J., & Talanov, M. (2017). Naturalizing Consciousness Emergence for AI Implementation Purposes: A Guide to Multilayered Management Systems. In J. Vallverdú, M. Mazzara, M. Talanov, S. Distefano, & R. Lowe (Eds.), *Advanced Research on Biologically Inspired Cognitive Architectures* (pp. 24–40). Hershey, PA: IGI Global. doi:10.4018/978-1-5225-1947-8.ch002

von Kutzleben, M., & Panke-Kochinke, B. (2015). Stable Self-Concepts and Flexible Coping Strategies of People with Dementia Attending Dementia Self-Help Groups in Germany: Results from the Qualitative Longitudinal SEIN Study. In C. Dick-Muehlke, R. Li, & M. Orleans (Eds.), *Psychosocial Studies of the Individual's Changing Perspectives in Alzheimer's Disease* (pp. 159–182). Hershey, PA: IGI Global. doi:10.4018/978-1-4666-8478-2.ch007

Vorkapić, S. T. (2017). Personality and Education: Contemporary Issues in Psychological Science about Personality in Teacher Education. In C. Martin & D. Polly (Eds.), *Handbook of Research on Teacher Education and Professional Development* (pp. 163–186). Hershey, PA: IGI Global. doi:10.4018/978-1-5225-1067-3.ch009

Wagner, C., & Schlough, D. E. (2017). Creativity: A Childhood Essential. In N. Silton (Ed.), *Exploring the Benefits of Creativity in Education, Media, and the Arts* (pp. 1–25). Hershey, PA: IGI Global. doi:10.4018/978-1-5225-0504-4.ch001

Wang, L., Li, C., & Wu, J. (2017). The Status of Research into Intention Recognition. In J. Wu (Ed.), *Improving the Quality of Life for Dementia Patients through Progressive Detection, Treatment, and Care* (pp. 201–221). Hershey, PA: IGI Global. doi:10.4018/978-1-5225-0925-7.ch010

Wehle, M., Weidemann, A., & Boblan, I. W. (2017). Research on Human Cognition for Biologically Inspired Developments: Human-Robot Interaction by Biomimetic AI. In J. Vallverdú, M. Mazzara, M. Talanov, S. Distefano, & R. Lowe (Eds.), *Advanced Research on Biologically Inspired Cognitive Architectures* (pp. 83–116). Hershey, PA: IGI Global. doi:10.4018/978-1-5225-1947-8.ch005

Wilson, J. G. (2017). Social Psychology: The Seduction of Consumers. In C. Martins & M. Damásio (Eds.), *Seduction in Popular Culture, Psychology, and Philosophy* (pp. 206–231). Hershey, PA: IGI Global. doi:10.4018/978-1-5225-0525-9.ch010

Wu, F., Tang, X., Ren, Y., Yang, W., Takahashi, S., & Wu, J. (2017). Effects of Visual Contrast on Inverse Effectiveness in Audiovisual Integration. In J. Wu (Ed.), *Improving the Quality of Life for Dementia Patients through Progressive Detection, Treatment, and Care* (pp. 187–200). Hershey, PA: IGI Global. doi:10.4018/978-1-5225-0925-7.ch009

Wu, Z., Lin, T., Tang, N., & Wu, S. (2015). Effects of Display Characteristics on Presence and Emotional Responses of Game Players. In A. Mesquita & C. Tsai (Eds.), *Human Behavior, Psychology, and Social Interaction in the Digital Era* (pp. 130–145). Hershey, PA: IGI Global. doi:10.4018/978-1-4666-8450-8.ch006

Xie, T., Zhu, Y., Lin, T., & Chen, R. (2015). Modeling Human Behavior to Reduce Navigation Time of Menu Items: Menu Item Prediction Based on Markov Chain. In A. Mesquita & C. Tsai (Eds.), *Human Behavior, Psychology, and Social Interaction in the Digital Era* (pp. 162–187). Hershey, PA: IGI Global. doi:10.4018/978-1-4666-8450-8.ch008

Related Readings

Yang, C., Ha, L., Yun, G. W., & Chen, L. (2015). From Relationship to Information: A Study of Twitter and Facebook Usage in Terms of Social Network Size among College Students. In A. Mesquita & C. Tsai (Eds.), *Human Behavior, Psychology, and Social Interaction in the Digital Era* (pp. 241–258). Hershey, PA: IGI Global. doi:10.4018/978-1-4666-8450-8.ch012

Yartey, F. N., & Ha, L. (2015). Smartphones and Self-Broadcasting among College Students in an Age of Social Media. In A. Mesquita & C. Tsai (Eds.), *Human Behavior, Psychology, and Social Interaction in the Digital Era* (pp. 95–128). Hershey, PA: IGI Global. doi:10.4018/978-1-4666-8450-8.ch005

About the Author

Shigeki Sugiyama has been working on various fields from Industrial Engineering, Control, Artificial Intelligence, Neural Networking, Virtual Reality, E-Learning, Embedded Technology, Computer, to Consciousness Studies for more than 30 years and has presented more than 80 papers. He has also put much attention on Service Science, especially on a network behavior in a scalable situation and has touched upon setting up a science park project about the matters of IT during 1994 – 1999 and has done some cooperative research works with universities in US and in Europe in Information Technologies. He has been a lecturer at Gifu Univ. and was a lecturer at Nagoya Management Junior College. After retirement, he is an independent researcher. Dr. Eng. from University of Gifu.

Index

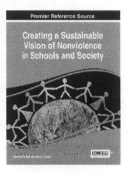

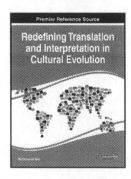

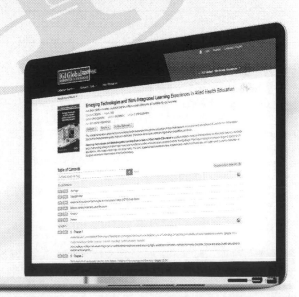